Why Not Say It Clearly:
A Guide to Expository Writing

Lester S. King, M.D.

Why Not Say It Clearly:
A Guide to Expository Writing

Second Edition

Little, Brown and Company
Boston/Toronto/London

Library of Congress Catalog Card No. 91-60017

ISBN 0-316-49353-8

Printed in the United States of America

SEM

Contents

Preface

"Of making many books there is no end." This well-known quotation from Ecclesiastes shows great insight. If there had also been greater foresight, the Preacher would have included, along with books, the periodicals, brochures, manuals, catalogues, memoranda, and documents that now threaten to overwhelm us. Even a casual sampling of all this reading matter shows that some is clear and easy to read, some confusing and hard to read. Such variation underlies the distinctions between "good" and "bad" writing. These terms, which express evaluation, are open to infinite dispute. Once we accept a distinction that some writing is "better" than others, the critical mind wants to know the basis on which this judgment rests. In this book I examine the concepts of good and bad writing and analyze the meanings that might attach to these terms.

We cannot regard the whole mass of written material as if it were a unit. Of the many possible modes of approach, I would start by inquiring about the *need* for good writing. How *important* is it? With this in mind I suggest three categories.

In the first we have the professional writer, who makes his living from his pen. If he is to survive, he must write well, for his livelihood depends on his writing skill. In a second group I place those whose livelihood depends primarily on activities other than writing, such as research, education, or medical practice, but for whom writing may play an accessory role. Teachers, for example, are paid primarily to teach and physicians primarily to heal the sick (or so, at least, it used to be thought). Teachers and physicians, however, may also want to write (for varied reasons that I will discuss later). In such endeavors we may say that writing skill has only incidental importance. A medical scientist, for example, who makes a great discovery, will gain recognition no matter how clumsy his modes of expression. Recognition depends on what he does, rather than on the skill with which he describes what he does. Nevertheless, those engaged in works of scholarship may find it advantageous to write well, depending on contextual factors that I will examine. By contrast, a bureaucrat, engaged in turning out streams of memoranda, may gain no advantage by writing clearly.

In this mode of subdivision we also have a third group, the vast mass of the population who have no real concern, economic or otherwise, with writing skills. They make their living in ways that do not involve written communication and they have no intrinsic aesthetic interest in the niceties of language. Hence, it makes no difference to anyone whether they write well.

In the total range of those who want to communicate—newspaper reporters, advertising executives, speech writers, public relations experts, bureaucrats, or members of professions whether learned or not so learned—we see different degrees of urgency for possessing writing skill. We can glimpse a vast range of contexts relevant to good or bad writing. The needs and values of the fiction writer, the politician, and the advertising executive are quite different. For ease of presentation I focus my discussion on the academic world.

Here the physician plays a key role, for he stands intermediate between the scientist on the one hand and the humanist on the other. The difficulties attending medical writing extend equally to the sciences and the humanities. When I refer specifically to the physician and to medicine, the import usually extends to disciplines like sociology, education, psychology, philosophy, history, and the like.

The first edition of this book had its inception in 1963 when I joined the editorial staff of the *Journal of the American Medical Association* (JAMA). A few months after I started, Dr. John H. Talbott, then editor, asked me to organize a course in medical writing for medical students. After the first year, Dr. Charles Roland, then newly appointed senior editor, became associated with the project, which expanded to include residents and practicing physicians. With the occasional help of outside teachers, we gave numerous courses, the longest of which lasted six weeks, the shortest, one day. Most satisfactory were the workshops that lasted one week.

After a few years, Dr. Roland and I embodied our experiences in a series of brief articles, first published in JAMA and later collected in a small volume entitled *Scientific Writing* (American Medical Association, 1966). Dr. Roland left the AMA shortly thereafter. *Scientific Writing* had been a joint enterprise. After a few years I found that the parts I had written no longer adequately expressed my ideas. Drawing on further experience I recast and rewrote the work, retaining some of the original examples, but producing what was essentially an entirely new book. This was the first edition of *Why Not Say It Clearly* (1978).

The book expressed my personal credo and did not in any way reflect the editorial policies of the American Medical Association or of any editorial board. I presented my own views on the nature of good writing and bad writing and the ways to achieve the one and avoid the other. With the passage of a dozen years and the resulting increased experience, I realized that the concepts could be made more clear and the perspective more cogent. I welcome the opportunity to bring out a new edition.

Originally Dr. Roland and I were concerned with the improvement of writing oriented toward science, with special reference to medicine, a goal expressed in the original subtitle of the book. However, the principles extend to all types of expository writing, whether describing what was said or done, offering directions for any procedure, presenting data from whichever field (whether medicine, sociology, history, or philosophy), providing explanations, or defending theories. All these come under the heading of expository writing.

A few words about the examples that I use. That most of them have a medical flavor merely reflects my editorial experience, which relates chiefly to medical manuscripts. The principles and recommendations are, I believe, entirely general, applicable to all kinds of expository writing.

With a few obvious exceptions, these examples are all real, some of them going back into the seventeenth century. When contemporary selections embody various faults, I carefully shield the authorship. I change the dates and numbers, and often the technical terms, like the names of disease conditions. All personal names are changed to Doe and Roe, whether John or Richard or Jane. Despite these changes, I carefully preserve the grammatical or stylistic faults for which the examples were originally chosen, and I never intensify an error to make the example more striking. On the contrary, if the excerpt had contained more than one problem, I might, for better pedagogic effect, correct all but the fault under discussion. However bad the quotations in the book might seem, the original texts were at least as bad, and often worse.

Older illustrative material, ordinarily in the public domain, does not need to be shielded. For such material, my references are deliberately casual and not pedantic.

By virtue of appearing in print, what I advocate may serve as a reference and take on a certain respectability. I would emphasize, however, that I do not set myself up as an authority. In expressing my own views I try to make explicit certain linguistic choices and to recommend some in preference to others. I emphasize the reasons for my decisions. While I hope that many will agree with me, I will not quarrel with those who disagree. This book may serve as a guide and perhaps an instructional manual, but it is not intended as an "authority."

L.S.K.

Why Not Say It Clearly:
A Guide to Expository Writing

· 1 ·

The Present Scene

The Tradition of Bad Writing

That an occasional physician should write obscurely is only to be expected. Paracelsus in the sixteenth century, van Helmont in the seventeenth, and John Hunter in the eighteenth are prime examples. Even their contemporaries noted difficulties in understanding what they were trying to say, and their lack of clarity has bothered historians ever since. But only in nineteenth-century America did critics indict virtually the whole medical profession for bad writing. Some readers might hold that the indictment remains in force today.

In the nineteenth century the United States was expanding rapidly, with a corresponding increase in the number of medical schools and practicing physicians. Many of these were poorly trained. When the American Medical Association was founded in 1847, it hoped to improve standards of medical education as well as practice. The annual *Transactions* of the association published various committee reports that richly illustrate the problems and comprise indispensable primary source material.

One of the standing committees dealt with "medical literature." While special attention was paid to the contents of the publications, many of this committee's reports commented on the style of writing. In 1850, for example, Alfred Stillé (1813–1900) deplored the "evidences of haste." This, however, was the least of the faults mentioned. Too often the style "is chargeable with all the mortal sins which the canons of criticism forbid; it sets at defiance grammar, rhetoric, and logic." We must conclude, he said, "that they who use their native tongue so awkwardly can hardly be accomplished expounders of science."

In scientific writing, he declared, that "the simplest form of

1

expression, that which renders the ideas most distinctly visible, is undoubtedly best." The style should have "such transparent simplicity that the reader scarcely feels it as a barrier between his mind and the author's." But while praising a simple style, he also pointed out that much truth might still be "veiled in the coarse texture of a rude and obscure style." He realized what is still true today, that a badly written paper may still have scientific merit. He also pointed out that, conversely, fine rhetoric may conceal poverty of thought.

Many of the early committee reports expanded these criticisms and elaborated on the bad writing of journal publications. In the 1853 report Nathan Smith Davis, later the first editor of *JAMA*, noted four major reasons for the defects. First was inadequate "preliminary education"; second, an inadequate grasp of the basic sciences (at that time chiefly physiology and pathology); third, "defective modes of investigation," including the failure to analyze, observe, and interpret. Today we would call this fault an inadequate grasp of scientific method. Fourth was excessive haste in preparing articles for publication.

The history of American medical journalism is a fascinating topic on which I can only touch. Suffice to note that many of the defects still troublesome today have had a continuous and fully recognized existence for a century and a half.

In the earlier nineteenth century medical writing comprised the major segment of American scientific literature and offers the best examples for specific critiques. By the late twentieth century many of the defects had spread to other branches of scholarly endeavor: The same factors that influenced medicine have also affected other areas of exposition.

Why Do Doctors Write So Much?

In 1900 an editorial in *JAMA* declared, "The number of articles submitted for publication could be cut down one-half, and not a thought eliminated in so doing" [1]. Today, almost a century later, many critics would still subscribe to this sentiment. Why, then, such a passion to write? The answer involves the social and economic fabric of both medicine and science.

Publication has always led to professional advancement. The impulse to publish stems from many sources. Relatively few persons have the intense investigative drive that compels them to carry on research. We think of Bichat or Magendie, Claude Bernard or Virchow or Koch, for whom research was the very breath of life. They could not *not* engage in research—and publication. Most physicians, however, are less endowed with talent and drive. Nevertheless, by recording their observations they might bring themselves to the attention of their colleagues and obtain thereby both the personal satisfaction of achievement and the additional benefit of professional advancement.

The earlier American medical literature consisted largely of clinical observations—case reports—together with variable amounts of theoretical discussion. In Europe, however, a major transformation was taking place, namely, the increase in experimentation (in contrast to description alone). This movement, which had been gaining momentum since the seventeenth century, reached explosive force in the nineteenth. Studies in anatomy, physiology, chemistry, pathology, and pharmacology provided a new "scientific" dimension to medical practice.

Clinical observations and descriptions lay well within the scope of capable practitioners. Experimental research, however, demanded much more. It required not only extensive training but money and special laboratory facilities as well, both of which, in mid-century America, were in short supply.

The way that these European currents entered American medicine and science, chiefly in the last half of the nineteenth century, and the effects thereby exerted, form a major aspect of medical history. The details I cannot discuss here but I will note only those end results that bear on medical writing.

Although ambitious practitioners could continue descriptive research, experimental work became associated with medical schools and foundations, that is, academia. Physicians interested in research wanted to associate themselves with academia, and in so doing they acquired a definite prestige. Certain tensions arose between academic and nonacademic practitioners, and also within the academic community itself. In all of this, medical publications played a significant role.

Beginning about 1870, amidst complex social and professional changes, the fateful academic imperative "publish or perish" gradually took shape. This dictum has had marked influence on medical writing.

The Multiplication of Journals

Authors and editors live in symbiosis, since each requires the other. Journals cannot exist without manuscripts; unpublished manuscripts accomplish nothing for their authors. Each symbiont, however, shows a wide range of characteristics. Journals vary in certain obvious respects: sponsoring organizations, intended audience, degree of specialization, circulation, frequency of appearance, competence of the editor, amount and quality of advertising, and, of considerable importance, prestige. Among authors, variables of special relevance would include professional competence as well as skill in writing.

The sponsors or publishers may represent segments of "organized medicine" on the county, state, or national level; or perhaps a professional specialty group (whether preclinical or clinical); or some organization pursuing special aims. To provide additional avenues of publication, many hospitals and medical schools also sponsor journals, as do some research foundations and government agencies.

The many thousands of medical journals may be categorized in various ways. Some are general, others specialized. The circulation may be large or small. Some have a worldwide reputation, others are unknown outside a limited circle. Some prosper, others lead a hand-to-mouth existence. They all need manuscripts.

In earlier days, scientific discoveries, if substantial, were published as books. If less profound or extensive, the results of research were circulated in letters, addressed to interested colleagues. Journals met the need for publication of short communications. When, however, more manuscripts were produced than existing journals could publish, new journals would appear.

Aiding the process of multiplication was the great increase in specialization. Physicians who specialized sometimes had trouble getting publication in the existing journals that had a more general character. Sooner or later the specialists established their own journals, appealing to an audience limited in numbers but strongly interested in the restricted subject matter. The production of manuscripts kept outrunning the facilities for publication, even within relatively narrow fields.

The Quest for Bibliography

The desire to publish and amass a bibliography may be an insidious addiction in anyone, but for academics it can reach crucial intensity. This results from two interrelated factors: the proverbial dictum, publish or perish, and the prevalence of grants as an aid to research. In the American intellectual climate the effect of grants, whether governmental or private, can scarcely be overestimated.

In a less sophisticated era, when the imperative publish or perish had less intensity, academics nevertheless encountered abundant difficulties. Radical changes occurred after World War II, when the research grant provided assistance, on a scale at first relatively modest and then becoming increasingly massive. For the individual scientist the whole business (the word is used advisedly) of grants embodied a magnificent circularity.

A list of publications made it easier to secure a grant. This new funding, by subsidizing further research, made it easy to amass a larger bibliography, and this in turn led more readily to additional grants. In the scramble to get financial assistance there was enormous pressure to get papers into print. There was no comparable pressure to advance good writing.

Academics of all types were caught up in a vicious circle. Many educational institutions, for example, were quite dependent on the grants that their faculty members could attract. The research grant became a sort of largess, which supported (at least in part) more and more institutions, which in turn produced more and more manuscripts. And, since unpublished manuscripts are singularly ineffective, more journals came into existence.

The academic world was seeing increasing numbers of research workers, producing increasing numbers of manuscripts, which exerted increasing pressure to achieve publication. Somewhere in this expanding micro-universe lies the need for clear writing. How important is this need?

What Journals and Authors Want

Although journals and authors live in symbiosis each group has different needs. Authors chafe at the long periods of delay before they learn whether their papers are accepted or rejected or, as is so often the case, sent back for revision. As a class authors pursue several distinct values. They want a journal that has a high prestige, gives a prompt decision regarding acceptance or rejection, publishes promptly, and reaches the audience in which the author is interested. Some journals, for example, may take six months or even more before coming to a decision. This may result from obsessive views regarding quality, together with demands for repeated revisions. Or, at fault may be sloppy administrative or editorial procedures. Then, some journals, after deciding to accept, may not publish the paper for as long as two years.

While an author hopes for prompt acceptance by a prestigious journal and the prompt publication that will reach the audience with which he is concerned, the journal editor, on the other hand, has a different set of values. His aim is to have on hand a comfortable backlog of good papers, sufficient to ensure a regular schedule but not so great as to delay the publication of new manuscripts. He wants a constant influx of new papers from which he can choose the "best." Only if he has an abundance from which to choose can he select what he wants and reject the rest.

A high rejection rate is, in a sense, an index of prestige. When many authors submit their work to a given journal, they indicate their high regard. Indeed, I might suggest an operative definition of prestige: Of competing journals that publish work in a given field, the one in which most authors would like to have their work appear would have the higher prestige. If a large number of manuscripts is submitted to a prestigious journal, a high rate of rejection necessarily follows.

This topic of prestige has a special relevance to both research grants and the strivings for academic advancement. The urge to publish has had prolific results, but mere number of papers says nothing about their quality. How worthy are they? How significant? The academia that encouraged the lust for bibliography is facing unexpected problems.

One sinister effect is the occasional actual fraud that takes place—the "fudging" of results, even in institutions of high reputation. In recent years such cheating has been publicized in the professional and lay press, as well as on television. While the number of proven examples is small, they have acted like a cancer in the scientific community

Another undesirable side effect is the practice known as multiple publication. The results of a research project might be divided into many parts, each of which is sent to a different journal. By subdividing a single project and spreading the results into many journals, authors can enlarge their bibliographies. Under some circumstance, of course, multiple publication makes good sense. When authors from different disciplines cooperate, their work may have different implications for their respective specialties. Each author wants to bring his studies to the attention of his own professional colleagues. To provide an appropriate focus for his own peer group, his presentation might differ from that of his collaborator.

Peer Review

Journals were facing the problem that in other areas was called quality control. In an earlier period the editor evaluated the merits of a paper and took full responsibility for acceptance or rejection. While he usually felt sufficiently expert to rely on his own judgment, he would ordinarily have an editorial board on which he might call for further opinion, should he so desire.

Research, however, developed so massively and in so many specialized directions that the expertise of any single person was soon rendered inadequate. While at all times even the most learned editor would sometimes ask outside experts for help, this procedure became more and more routine. Finally the concept arose—at least in some journals—that all manuscripts should be reviewed by supposed experts in the subject matter at hand.

No editorial board could be large enough to include experts on all aspects of medicine in their innumerable minute subdivisions. If all manuscripts are to be reviewed by such experts, an editor may have to go far afield to find someone of the appropriate competence. This difficulty has given rise to the concept of "peer review"—that a manuscript is to be evaluated by the acknowledged *peers* of the authors.

Peer review has been defined as "the assessment of work by outside experts." Stephen Lock has provided an acute analysis, and a subsequent symposium, sponsored by the American Medical Association, has greatly expanded the subject [2,3]. The whole subject ramifies into areas quite remote from our present interests, and I will limit myself to a few aspects particularly relevant to medical writing and scientific communication.

A good editor, it has been said, can *smell* out a promising paper, and even more readily a bad one. Of all the manuscripts that are ultimately rejected, an experienced editor can identify most of them out of hand, without bothering about reviewers. Similarly, he recognizes good manuscripts, even though he may want help in evaluating certain technical features. There remain a certain number, however, about whose merits he is unsure and on which he will seek outside advice.

With highly technical subjects an editor will feel more comfortable if he can depend on the decision of a committee rather than on his own judgment. With controversial topics, too, the institution of peer review allows the sharing of responsibility. Peer review, however, when universally applied, seems nothing more than a fetish, and a boast of an allegedly highly critical attitude.

A good reviewer performs many of the functions of an editor. Since a journal may have on hand a listing of several thousand potential reviewers, all alleged experts in various fields, there would thus seem to be a roster of several thousand editors. In journals obsessed with the peer review system, the emphasis can lie on what the reviewer says rather than on the opinions of the editorial staff, however knowledgeable. Younger editors, instead of strengthening their own critical judgment, learn to depend on reviewers. Actually, among reviewers, true expertise can be quite narrow. A reviewer, competent in a limited area, may be asked to pass judgment on a paper that falls outside his proven abilities. Unwarranted deference can be paid to the opinions of outsiders, chiefly because they are outsiders.

The problem involves the question of whether the reviewer is truly the peer of the author. This is more likely to be the case in a journal of quite limited subject matter. The more general the scope of the journal, and the wider the range of articles submitted, the less likely is the editor to know the real qualifications of his consultants relative to any particular paper. Thus, when policy dictates that outside opinion is indispensable, the editor handling the paper may have only a foggy notion of how well qualified an alleged "peer" may be.

Used with discretion, peer review can enhance confidence in a publication. Used indiscriminately, the process can lead to an expensive, time-consuming bureaucratic routine that eventually will be self-defeating.

If the system of peer review expands unduly, we can, perhaps, imagine the editorial work of the future. A skillful secretary, after identifying the proper category for a manuscript, draws on the computer for listed experts, gets them to review the paper, and then presents the results to one or two decision makers.

Unfortunately, when "peer review" represents a shibboleth, less and less attention is paid to good writing. Reviewers attend primarily to the content of a paper, and if they stray into linguistic niceties, their opinions may be poorly grounded. All too often the editors themselves have only modest writing skills, so that making a manuscript more readable, a basic function of an editor, may then fall to a copy editor who lacks technical knowledge. Because of this lack, authors may legitimately object to some changes. As a result, editorial prudence may dictate a policy of "light editing," that is, the copy editor should correct for house style and eliminate glaring errors, but otherwise let the author write the way he wants.

Clarity and grace do not then have a high priority. With such a usage a journal may gradually become more and more opaque.

The whole institution of peer review has extremely complex origins, ranging from the rapid expansion of science to various socioeconomic factors. While the process does smooth out certain difficulties, it also intensifies certain others.

The Role of Advertising

One economic factor that has influenced medical writing deserves recognition. All publication is expensive, but journals differ markedly from books. With a book, a product that can be marketed like any other product, the cost is met chiefly through direct sales. Sometimes subsidies, direct or indirect, also help to defray costs (or in occasional instances pay the entire cost). With medical and other so-called learned periodicals, the direct or "over-the-counter" sales are negligible and thus the subscription has special importance.

Although some journals defray expenses solely from subscription revenues (to which subsidies may occasionally be added), others depend on advertising. Journals with a large circulation can derive huge revenues from advertising, but many complications may arise therefrom. I will mention only two.

The first concerns the category known as the "controlled circulation" journals. These represent a profit-making venture. They are sent free, but only to a restricted and relatively homogeneous group. Because their distribution is quite selective, the advertising can be precisely directed and presumably will have a higher effectiveness than with a more general audience.

Since the reader pays nothing, all costs are defrayed by the advertising receipts. Such publications, however, must be *readable* to compete successfully for the attention of the reader and thus bring about exposure of the advertising matter. To assure a high readership the editor must secure text articles that are appealingly written so that the advertising may have an attentive audience.

Such journals are sometimes called "throwaways." They vary widely in their principal interest. Some try to review new scientific advances and render them more intelligible and readable than did the original publications. Other such journals focus on socioeconomic issues, still others on more literary and cultural features. The throwaways may flourish vigorously, but they will disappear if their advertising revenues dry up.

The authors who contribute to these journals must write well. Indeed, when compared with the "regular" medical periodicals, the level of writing is conspicuously higher. Nevertheless, the throwaway journals do not carry academic prestige. The authors who contribute to such journals do not advance up the academic ladder.

Advertising also influences medical journals in a quite different way. Periodicals, to qualify for favorable postal rates, must not exceed a specified ratio of advertising matter to editorial content. If advertisements exceed this ratio, higher postal rates apply—a potential financial disaster. Hence, in boom times, when a journal carries increased advertising, there must be a corresponding increase in quantity of editorial matter. The postal service is not at all fussy regarding what publishers designate as editorial matter. Sometimes mere "filler" will satisfy the requirements, but conscientious editors will print more leading articles.

The available backlog of accepted papers may get used up at a frightening rate, even as the need for additional ones expands inexorably. Since the editor must find further textual matter, the standards for acceptance and publication may get lowered.

On the other hand, if advertising revenues shrink, the journal must correspondingly restrict its editorial content and be more rigorous in what it accepts. In journals financially dependent on advertising, mammon plays a subtle, and sometimes not so subtle, role.

In the field of medical publication we can glimpse a tangled sequence. A journal may want to attract advertisers. Important in this quest is a high circulation. To attract readers the contents must be readable; to increase prestige they must be significant. In all this, is there a place for sound, clear writing? Just what this place might be is by no means clear. I have pointed to many

11

difficulties and raised many questions, without offering any answers. The answers must come from the editors themselves when they possess a heightened literary conscience.

References

1. Editorial. *JAMA* 35:626, 1900.
2. Stephen Lock. *A Different Balance: Edditorial Peer Review in Medicine.* Philadelphia: ISI Press, 1986.
3. Twenty four papers of this symposium were published in *JAMA* 283:1317–1441 (*passim*), 1990.

· 2 ·

Good and Bad Writing: Orientation

Standards

When we declare that some writings are better than others, we are implying standards, implicit or explicit. We are relying on a scale of values, with the relatively good at one end, the relatively bad at the other. When we evaluate particular examples and place them at different levels of our scale, what is it that makes *this* better than *that?* What are the criteria by which we judge? Who sets these standards? What compulsion do they exert?

In the seventeenth century Cardinal Richelieu established the French Academy, one of whose functions was to set official standards for the French language. What the academy approved was good, what it condemned was bad. In England, which had no comparable official monitors, the closest approach to a formal authority for language was a dictionary. Of the earlier works of this genre, that of Samuel Johnson is the best known. Since his time a dictionary has continued to serve as arbiter of spelling and meaning.

Modern dictionaries also serve to define usage. They tell us whether a word is rare, obsolete, archaic, dialect, rude, vulgar, or slang. The dictionary thus indicates the acceptability of words. Those not found therein would have little or no validity in educated circles. The familiar four letter words were certainly widely used in rude speech, but were not admitted into the dictionary.

More recently the major dictionaries proclaimed a different function. They refused to be normative, that is, to set standards of good or bad, of better or worse. Instead, they exerted a descriptive function, indicating the language that was actually being used.

They did not try to distinguish good words from bad. As a result various words formerly rejected from polite discourse appeared in the dictionary.

When dictionaries stopped setting standards of good and bad, considerable uproar ensued. For many persons this abnegation of authority proved quite traumatic. If we cannot rely on some authority, how do we know what is correct or incorrect? Here we touch a fundamental question, namely, the role of authority in our culture. This topic I can approach only indirectly.

The meaning and selection of individual words form only one aspect of communication. Another deals with the way that words are put together. This, called syntax and grammar, is governed by definite rules, appropriately set out in grammar texts and taught in school.

Of course, before children get to school and learn to write, they already talk fluently. Their speech habits have already been formed. The early exposure to the spoken word largely determines speech habits and reflects cultural environment. But while speech is, so to speak, passively absorbed, writing must be specifically taught and deliberately learned through effort. Ordinarily this takes place in school.

Here teachers make a forceful distinction between correct and incorrect. In arithmetic, for example, a given answer is either right or wrong, with no intermediate stage. What is correct is automatically not-wrong; and what is not-wrong is automatically correct. In writing a different set of values applies, more comprehensive than the simple distinction of wrong or not-wrong.

In the study of "composition" we must recognize gradations of what is not-wrong. Something may be correct, so far as spelling, grammar, and syntax are concerned, but still capable of improvement. It can be made *better*. For clarification, I will examine some implications of what is "correct" and its relationships to context.

One aspect I will illustrate by analogy. Suppose you want to know the correct time. You look at your watch, but realizing that it may be slow, you want to check it. To do this you refer to the radio or the television, or perhaps the telephone service, or the chronometer in the jeweler's window. These will probably agree within reasonable limits, and you will consider them correct enough for practical purposes. You thus regard as the "right time" the answer given by the authority you accept for that particular context.

Some contexts, however, may raise difficulties. For example, the session of a state legislature must, according to statute, terminate at midnight on a given day. If midnight approaches and there is still a lot of unfinished business, the sergeant-at-arms may stop the clock while the legislature proceeds with its business. "Midnight" arrives only when the appropriate authority officially declares that it does. If the sergeant-at-arms says that the time is 11:45, it is quite irrelevant, *in that context,* that the radio signal says 5:00 A.M.

Admittedly, relatively few persons can thus stop the clock and get away with it. Nevertheless, within a limited context the right time is what some person, with suitable authority, *asserts* to be the right time. In some situations we have the option of rejecting that authority and seeking a different answer elsewhere. In other contexts, we have no options—the person making the assertion has authority backed by power, and if we do not believe him there is not much we can do about it.

I suggest a parallel between asserting the "right" time and evaluating the merits of writing. Different authorities may rely on different standards. Good writing is what some expert says is good, yet what one expert—whether lexicographer, grammarian, critic, teacher, or editor—says is good, another may reject. Furthermore, experts differ in the power they exert. Sometimes the authority is such that we have no recourse, but other times there are alternatives. A student who flunks out of school may be able to go to a different school. An author whose manuscript is rejected may send it elsewhere.

Teachers, of course, may be in error, and editors may exhibit poor judgment. Aspiring authors love to hear about any book manuscript that has been rejected by a dozen or so editors, and then, when eventually accepted, becomes a runaway best seller. There is often great satisfaction when supposed experts "get egg on their face." A more general statement would be that standards

15

vary according to time, place, and the person in authority. Standards are relative to context.

Standards and values relate to the whole cultural environment, which changes relatively slowly. As an example I would mention the culture of mid-Victorian England, so markedly different from that of the American frontier of the 1870s. We may compare either of them with the urban American culture of the 1920s—the "flapper" era. Such distinct cultural patterns we can construe as a sort of *zeitgeist* affecting behavior, thought, and communication. Their study forms part of social history in its broad sense.

Another type of context is narrow and local. It deals with particular situations as they affect the modes of speech or writing. Thus, the social conversation known as "small talk" differs in its characteristics from a speech given at a dedication ceremony; a letter to the family, written on vacation, differs from a letter of condolence. When we consider what is "appropriate" (i.e., "proper"), the particular circumstances and intended audience must govern our evaluations. In forming our critical judgments we must keep in mind the context and distinguish between a broad cultural environment and narrow local circumstances. What is considered acceptable in one situation could be deemed unsuitable in another.

Developing a Critical Sense

When I gave courses in writing, I emphasized that "good" and "bad" were relative terms. Calling some writing bad meant that it had many faults and sorely needed improvement. Calling another example good did not mean that it could not stand improvement, but that its present form was quite satisfactory. It did not cry aloud for change. The criterion was simple: If we did make changes, would the result be *better* than the original? And then, how do we decide? In my classes the students (and in this book, the readers) would be the judges.

My first goal was to help the students discriminate between good and bad, in the senses noted above. The second goal was to help

16

them acquire techniques for turning relatively bad writing into something better. If they could do this for the writings of others, they would be able to apply the principles to their own manuscripts. I wanted them to acquire a critical sense. In practice I gave a few examples which I asked the class to categorize as relatively good or relatively bad, without further qualification. The examples were carefully chosen, and usually the students agreed on most of the judgments. But then I would ask the truly difficult question, *Why* do you call some good and some bad? The students had to defend their opinions. The comments were usually quite indefinite, with terms like *unclear* or *confused,* for those examples judged bad, and *interesting* or *informative,* for those judged good. The students had an intuitive reaction but could not analyze the reasons that induced the particular judgments.

I then tried to provide an analytic framework to help them justify their decisions. Naturally, I offered my own scheme of values, which they were free to accept or modify as they chose. But in presenting my own viewpoint I always stressed the reasons behind my opinions, and if the students disagreed, I insisted that they formulate reasons.

Here I give three representative examples of what I offered for evaluation. The first comes from a publication in neuropsychiatry, the second from a book review, the third from a real estate advertisement. Two I characterize as bad, the other as relatively good.

The results of the present study suggest that in addition to the manifestation of aberrant homeostatic patterns of neurohumoral activity following the cessation of noxious stimulation, the neurotic may be further characterized by atypical autonomic responses to an increase in the level of appetitional drives.

The book is essentially a potboiler. Although abundant research has gone into it, the text is largely scissors-and-paste—excerpts taken from contemporary sources and joined together by facile prose. No real picture emerges. There is no synthesis. The author has not digested anything. We do not get a real three-dimensional picture of the times; we do not get any insight into the medical practice of the era; we learn neither American history nor medical history; and we are not very much entertained.

The unique old world charm in scenic country-like atmosphere with a large variety of individualistic newer as well as charming older homes of various styles on larger wooded parcels makes Lake County the favorite of a large number of Detroit executives.

Content, Form, and Judgment

Customarily we distinguish between content and form, between what we are trying to say and the way we say it. Whether these aspects are truly separable is, perhaps, an open question, and one to which we will return in a later chapter. For the present I will treat them as separable. The questions, How can you improve what you have said? and How can you make it better? refer to form. The notion of "better" implies not only standards but also the existence of techniques for meeting those standards. Specific details of technique I will consider later. Here I will take up only some general considerations.

As an editor I may receive a manuscript that conveys an important message, yet is so badly written as to be quite unpublishable. How to get it into suitable shape? Usually an author who produces a badly written paper does not know how to do better. I would not make his task easier if I recommended that he read some standard books on writing—full of good advice that is usually singularly unhelpful. Such books may tell him to eliminate redundancy, get rid of fancy words, avoid loose sentences, and use strong active verbs. But how will the poor author identify which words are needless, which sentences are loose, or which verbs are strong?

The writer who wants to improve his style must develop judgment regarding the values involved in writing. He must become sensitized to bad writing. He must constantly try to discriminate the good from the bad, whether he is reading a newspaper, a medical journal, a volume of history, a treatise in philosophy, or a textbook of pathology.

In bad writing, a characteristic warning flag is a difficulty in understanding what the author is trying to say. You may "stumble"

18

as you read, so that even when you know the meaning of each individual word, you fail to grasp the sense, or you arrive at it only after several readings. Of course, we are presupposing a certain level of maturity. A child might readily understand a topic discussed in a children's encyclopedia but not the account in a college textbook, no matter how well written the latter might be. But the mature and reasonably well educated adult who cannot understand expository writing should not conclude that he is dull-witted or that the subject is too abstruse for him. He should at least entertain the suspicion that the fault lies with the author and that the writing is bad. Alternatively, he may surmise that the author is somewhat confused, does not fully understand the subject, or is not clear about what he is trying to say. An author who knows his subject thoroughly and can write well should be able to make his exposition readily intelligible, even with an abstruse subject.

Writing is a skill, like golf. Some persons are naturally good at it, most are not, but all can improve with practice, especially if guided by proper instruction. In golf we have an objective measure of merit—the score—and the score can also serve as an index of improvement. In writing, there is no such objective measure. Nevertheless, good writing does differ from bad, and the more readily an aspiring author can recognize the bad, the more readily can he improve his own writing. He should become sensitized to certain major faults, so that when he encounters them they will engender acute discomfort—as if someone had rubbed sand on a fresh sunburn.

There is a perpetual dialectic in regard to standards—we crave them and yet we rebel against them. The critic—I use the term in its best sense—has the function of analyzing and justifying standards. Each reader of this book, I assume, will develop his own critical faculties and set his own standards. I enunciate my own values, with the hope that readers will agree. The important factor is the remedy—the alternative pathways that can lead to better writing.

My approach is the empirical presentation of alternatives, and the reasons that underlie them. Does a given passage read smoothly and easily? If not, how to make it smoother? The precepts that I offer I have used in editing and teaching, and in this book I try to make them explicit. The reader should adopt them only if he is convinced that they improve the writing. If he is not convinced, I have no quarrel with him.

There is, however, an important difference between editing a journal and teaching a course in writing. An editor has definite responsibilities, and to carry these out he must exert authority. In contrast, if a student in my writing courses was not convinced that my suggestions effected an improvement, I did not push the issue. This book does not pretend to assert any authority. I merely offer alternatives for the reader to accept or reject. In making his choice he is developing his own judgment. And this is what I want him to do.

· 3 ·

Back to Basics

Most small children enjoy playing with blocks—usually, simple cubes—and placing them in various spatial relationships. Later, some youngsters go on to play with large construction sets, whose elements, instead of being uniform, show different shapes and sizes and have various means of making connections with one another. Then the child soon realizes that different pieces have different functions.

We can make a rough analogy between learning to manipulate construction blocks and learning to use language. When playing with blocks, children first place the elements into simple relationships; in a similar manner they readily juxtapose words. But just as, when playing with complex construction sets, the youngsters must distinguish the separate elements and their various capabilities, so too they learn that words have different functions and enter into different relationships.

The different kinds of blocks I would compare to the parts of speech and their respective functions. With construction sets, after the child learns the different pieces and their possible relationships, he can make impressive and stable objects. Comparably, with language, the different kinds of words and their functions comprise grammar. This permits the child to establish useful and pleasing communication.

The parts of speech, in themselves, are entirely neutral and for their effect depend on the way in which they are put together. Used skillfully they have great power; used unskillfully, they can make the speech or writing clumsy and obscure. Parts of speech I would compare to servants who, while capable of fine work, may prove treacherous if not carefully watched.

In this chapter I will discuss some parts of speech—the elements of language—and the ways in which they can lead to trouble if not properly controlled. Since this is not a text of grammar, I am arbitrarily selective in what I choose to discuss. I will talk about verbs, especially the verb *to be*, prepositions, conjunctions, modifiers, and pronouns. For simplicity and convenience I symbolize these classes by single words, namely, *is*, *of*, *and*, *very*, and *it*. Well controlled, they are admirable servants. Without such control, they can wreck any composition.

IS, A SPECIAL VERB

Verbs express action: In the sentence "He hit the ball," a subject *he* performs the action *hit*, affecting an object, the *ball*. We call *hit* a transitive verb because it takes an object. On the other hand, in the sentence "He ran," the subject also performs an action but does not affect any object. The verb *ran* we call intransitive.

We also distinguish active from passive, thereby referring to a property we call *voice*. This indicates a particular relationship between subject and verb. If the subject is, so to speak, on the delivery end, as in the sentence "He hit the ball," we designate the verb as active or in the active voice. If the subject is on the receiving end, "He was hit by the ball," the verb is passive. The passive voice always includes some form of the verb *to be*, which serves as an auxiliary to the main verb.

To be stands apart from other verbs, for by itself it does not indicate any action. It may serve as an auxiliary, entering into compound verb forms, but any action depends entirely on the main verb. The auxiliary merely shows where the action of the main verb lies. We appreciate this if we recall that in Latin we express the passive voice by a grammatical inflection, without any distinction of main and auxiliary verbs. Where Latin uses a verb ending, English uses an auxiliary.

A further use of *to be* as an auxiliary we find in the so-called progressive or continuing form of a verb. "He was walking" tells us something rather different from the simple "He walked," for it makes explicit the continuity of an action, namely, a progression. In Latin this sense is conveyed through a specific ending, that is, through an inflection of the verb. English, as a poorly inflected language, must use another mode of expressing the same idea, and does so by combining an auxiliary verb with the participle. The latter reveals the activity while the auxiliary replaces the case ending found in the Latin. The progressive forms of a verb—is walking, was walking, had been walking—can thus give precise shades of meaning.

To be also functions as a *copula,* a junction word that joins the subject to another term that the grammarians call the *subject complement.* Thus, in the two sentences "John Doe is tall" and "John Doe is the author," the *is* links John Doe in the one case with an adjective, in the other with a noun. As copula the *is* makes explicit the relationship between subject and complement but does not itself contribute to the relationship, nor does it limit either term, nor, of course, does it express any action.

In the discussion of *to be* I will consider its function as copula and as auxiliary in the passive voice, for these are the functions whose abuse makes so much prose so dull and flabby. I will not take up the use of the progressive form.

If we want to eliminate a major component of bad writing, namely, the excessive use of *to be,* we must first become sensitive to the deadly quality of the prose in which this excess occurs. Read the following quotation aloud and stress slightly the words in italics. (The quotation refers to the serum calcium levels under certain conditions of hyperparathyroidism.)

> The serum calcium level *is* constantly elevated. However, there *is* no change in protein binding, and measurement of total calcium *is* as useful as measurement of any fraction. Hypercalciuria *is* usually present, but *is* not useful as a sign, since it *is* abolished if glomerular filtration *is* impaired, as it *is* in many cases of hyperparathyroidism.

This passage contains eight verbs, all of them embodying some form of the verb *to be* either as a simple copula or as part of a passive verb.

Take this further example.

> This small monograph *is* an excellent summary of current concepts of neurophysiology. It *is* profusely illustrated with beautiful pictures and clear diagrams. The text *is* relatively simple and *is* obviously written for the non-expert, for there *are* very few references cited.

These two sentences contain five verbs, in all of which some form of *to be* appears, twice as copula and three times as auxiliary in passive verbs. I maintain that these examples contain far too many instances of *is* and *are* forms and that if we eliminate most of these we will bring about an improvement: The sentences will be *better.* To indicate some ways to get rid of *to be* forms, I will consider the second example.

Surprisingly often we can simply omit the copula and bring the complement into direct contact with the subject. We may link an adjective directly to the subject and thus eliminate an *is.* Instead of saying "The text is relatively simple," we need merely say, "The relatively simple text" and then attach the subject, *text,* to some other verb. In the present example we say, "The relatively simple text is obviously written. . . ." One *is* has disappeared, along with an *and.*

Another common technique converts a noun complement into a verb: "*is* a summary" becomes *summarizes:* "This small monograph summarizes current concepts. . . ." What, then do we do with the *excellent* that originally modified *summary?* We convert it into an adverb that modifies *summarizes,* so that *excellent summary* becomes *excellently summarizes.* "This small monograph excellently summarizes current concepts. . . ." Another *is* has disappeared, along with the preposition *of.*

A further technique involves some combinations and transformations. In the sentence, "It is profusely illustrated. . . ," the *it* refers to *monograph* in the preceding sentence. This new bit of information we can transpose back to the first sentence and attach it directly to the subject *monograph.* In so doing we eliminate both the *it* and the *is.* The transformation gives us, "Profusely illustrated with beautiful pictures and clear diagrams, this small monograph. . . ." Another copula has vanished, along with an unnecessary pronoun.

There remain three *is* forms—one copula and two passives. Eliminating one of the passive constructions would continue the improvement. To accomplish this we must make the grammatical subject into the grammatical object, thus placing the former subject on the receiving end, so to speak, of the verb *cite*. "There are very few references cited" turns into ". . . cites very few references." What, then, is the grammatical subject? What agent does the citing? Obviously, *the text*. But since the word *text* has already occurred in the main clause, we can use the pronoun *it* in the subordinate clause: "for it [the text] cites very few references."

If we put all this together we find that the revision reads:

Profusely illustrated with beautiful pictures and clear diagrams, this small monograph summarizes excellently the current concepts of neurophysiology. The text, relatively simple, is obviously written for the nonexpert, for it cites very few references.

We now have three verbs, two of them active and one passive, and no copulas at all. We have eliminated four of the original five instances of *to be*. Is not the revision better than the original?

I have no intrinsic objection to the passive voice or to the copula. I object only to their excessive use. The copula, instead of adding something of its own, merely fulfills a grammatical need to make a complete sentence. Even though sometimes indispensable, the copula remains an "empty" word. Hence, too many copulas dilute the sense. Since empty words automatically exclude vigorous expressive verbs, they may lead to bovine monotony and flabby writing. The passive voice may sometimes provide the exact shade of meaning that the author intends, but overabundant use indicates slipshod habits of writing, combining ignorance, carelessness, and laziness. More rarely, excessive use of the passive voice stems from adherence to standards that in my opinion are utterly wrong, as I will explain later.

What constitutes an excess? I suggest a rule of thumb: In any given segment of writing, no more than one-fourth to one-third of the verbs should be copulas or passives. For those persons willing to make a substantial effort to improve their writing, I suggest the following exercise. Choose eight to ten consecutive sentences from any random text and count the total number of verbs. Record this as the denominator of a fraction. Then count the copulas or passives and record that number as the numerator. If the fraction exceeds one-third, consider the number of copulas as excessive. If you are examining your own writing, try to eliminate as many of the passives or copulas as you can. (Please note that I do not include the progressive forms of verbs, for these usually contribute to precision and vigor rather than detract therefrom.)

In the following additional examples wherein copulas or passives can be eliminated with advantage, notice one particular warning flag, which I call the *is-and construction*. This we have already encountered. Here is another instance.

Man *is* a part of nature *and* shares in the phenomena that apply to all other animals.

If we delete both the *is* and the *and,* and insert commas in their places, we have an improved sentence. For the sake of euphony we can insert an *as,* so that the sentence reads,

Man, as part of nature, shares in the phenomena that apply to all other animals.

Again,

The second part of the text *is* directed to clinical pathology *and* begins with a general discussion of apparatus.

Delete both the *is* and the *and* and insert commas, turning the sentence into,

The second part of the text, devoted to clinical pathology, begins with a discussion of apparatus.

Or again,

The book *is* divided into three sections *and* consists of. . . .

becomes

The book, divided into three sections, consists of. . . .

Sometimes, when we start to get rid of an *is*, we find that we can spare other words as well. Thus:

The work that *is* represented in this book *is* a valuable contribution to physiology *and* will undoubtedly *be* widely used as a reference source.

Obviously, we can easily get rid of the first *is*, together with the accompanying *that*, to yield,

The work represented in this book *is* a valuable contribution. . . .

But do we lose anything if we chop a little more? *The work represented in* can readily disappear without loss of meaning and leave us with "This book. . . ." Then we can correct the *is-and* construction, and the original clumsy sentence becomes,

This book, a valuable contribution to physiology, will undoubtedly *be* widely used as a reference source.

Please note that we have not meddled with the passive voice *will be used.*

Another empty construction is the all-too-common usage, "The fact is that," "It is clear that," and similar clauses. These we should eliminate ruthlessly. Sometimes, to the resulting shortened version we can profitably add an adverb to render the sentence more euphonious and provide a better transition. Then a sentence such as,

The fact *is* that thieves *were* an important class in the total social structure

becomes

Indeed, thieves *were* an important class in the total social structure.

In regard to copulas, I strongly advocate the technique of changing the noun complement into a verb. In the sentence,

This excellent volume *is* a compilation of papers presented at a symposium

we can delted the *is* and turn *compilation* into the verb *compile*. Thus:

This excellent volume compiles the papers presented at a symposium.

But since the verb *compiles* demands a personal subject and *volume* is inanimate, we can change *compile* to *gather* or *bring together,* and say,

This excellent volume brings together the papers read at a symposium.

Sometimes the elimination of an *is* demands the insertion of a facilitating word such as *as* to cover a change in construction.

An unexpected feature of this book *is* the inclusion of a discussion on gynecological emergencies.

This would become:

> As an unexpected feature, this book includes a discussion of gynecological emergencies.

A sentence in the passive voice tells us that something has been or is being done. To indicate an agent we would need a prepositional phrase. A writer might say, "The book was written by me," a sentence whose meaning is clear but whose clumsiness would be hard to surpass. Yet we have no problem in converting it to the active voice: "I wrote the book."

Many times the passive construction does not tell us the identity of the agent, but allows us to presume it. Take this example, from a book review commenting on a recent volume on statistical method.

> The concept of randomization is stressed throughout as a key principle in design. However, the difficulty of achieving a true random sample is not fully discussed.

If we ask, Who does the stressing or the discussing? the answer is obviously the author of the book. We can improve the review by changing the passive to the active and making the agency explicit. At the same time we can make a few judicious transpositions and insertions.

> Throughout, the author stresses the concept of randomization as a key principle in design, even though he does not fully discuss the difficulty of achieving a true random sample.

Often, however, the identity of the agent remains unclear. In medical journals we constantly see statements that a problem was investigated, a patient was transferred, a catheterization was performed, and the like. To answer the question, Who did these things? we need to take account of certain additional factors. If, for example, the author declares, in the opening of his paper, that "the problem of blood flow was investigated," we must gather from the context whether he is referring to his own work—that he is the agent—or to the work of some other investigators. Ordinarily, but not always, the context allows us to make a clear decision. It would be far more helpful, however, if he said, "I [we] investigated. . ." or "Doe and Roe investigated. . . ."

Rather different is the sentence "The patient was transferred to the surgical service." Is the author referring to the physical transport of the patient, presumably performed by an orderly? If so, does it make any difference who actually moved the patient from one place to another? It would be otiose to make an explicit statement, "The orderly transferred the patient to the surgical service." If the author had in mind not the physical transport of the patient but the administrative transfer—the shift in responsibility from the physician to the surgeon—then the agent would presumably be some particular clerk making a suitable notation. But again, there is no point whatever in indicating the agent. The sentence "The patient was transferred to the surgical service" tells us all we need to know, and any effort to change the sentence to the active voice would be counterproductive.

The sentence "He was catheterized" might seem comparable. Indeed, if we are talking about the urinary bladder, it would make little difference who passed the catheter. But if we are talking about cardiac catheterization, we might want to know who actually performed the operation.

When we use the passive voice we must always consider whether the identity of the agent is significant to our story. Consider the following quotation.

> When the condition of a patient at the time of discharge was suggestive of an undiagnosed wound infection, an effort was made to trace the patient through local nursing homes and family physicians.

This sentence contains two verbs. The first, *was*, with its complement *suggestive of*, is certainly clear, even if clumsy. The natural mode of expression, however, would be "When the condition of the patient . . . suggested a wound infection. . . ." Torturing this into the passive voice indicates a virtual obsession that I will discuss shortly. In the second verb, "an effort *was made* to trace the patient. . .," the agent has considerable importance. *Who* tried to trace the patient? A trained social worker? A ward clerk? A surgical resident? Perhaps the author himself? Unless we know who made the effort, we have no way of evaluating the results. The passive voice can lead to ambiguity and doubts, as well as to clumsiness and monotony.

How can we account for the popularity of the passive voice? I suggest two major factors. The first relates to defects in our educational system. As various literary journals have complained, nowhere in our educational system are students taught to write. With rare exceptions, teachers and students alike avoid contact with English composition.

The second factor has to do with a mistaken notion about science and its relation to "scientific" communication. The alleged objectivity of science has hypnotized many otherwise capable scientists, who regard anything subjective as tainted, to be avoided as much as defective instruments or contaminated solutions. The logic is simple. The active voice will necessarily require abundant use of the first person—"I did this" or "We did that"; *I* and *we* are subjective, to be avoided as unscientific; the only alternative is the passive voice which, by avoiding the first person, becomes the favored mode of expression.

With this point of view I must disagree in the strongest possible terms. I maintain that objectivity in science is in large part a myth, and that if the devotees of this mythology would apply themselves to clear expression rather than to indefensible dogma, we would have a far greater general benefit.

I am reminded of a seminar in medical writing that I once gave to a group of residents. I pleaded for fewer passive constructions and greater use of the first person. When I had finished, several residents mentioned that the head of the department, who reviewed all manuscripts intended for publication, positively forbade any use of the first person. Everything had to be in the third person, even when a resident was applying for a research grant. Such a blanket rule, as it spreads the illusion of objectivity, also encourages use of the passive. All I can do is to exhort my readers not to follow this example.

Before we leave the verb *to be,* there is one further usage that deserves notice—the so-called absolute construction. This refers to the combination of a noun and a participle that together form a grammatical unit not connected with anything else in the sentence. The construciton is most familiar in Latin. Caesar would have said, "The town having been captured, the army crossed the river." "The town having been captured" translates an ablative absolute, *oppido capto* in which the noun in the ablative is combined with a past participle also in the ablative. These two words stand by themselves. This is good Latin, but a literal translation is not good English. An idiomatic translation might read, "After the town was captured, the army crossed the river."

From time to time we find the absolute construction in English. A book reviewer commented on a new edition of a book in a rather technical subspecialty. He declared,

> Therapeutics is but little changed from the previous edition, there having been no marked advance in the interim.

"There having been no marked advance" modifies nothing and stands by itself as an absolute. To bring it into relation with the rest of the sentence, we change the absolute to a subordinate clause: "for there have been no marked advances in the interim."

A further example describes a contemporary physician.

> Like his colleagues, he was famed for his skillful knowledge of cardiac disorders, his name being associated with heart block.

This we change to ". . . skillful knowledge of cardiac disorders, especially in relation to heart block." There are, of course, many different transformations possible, just as there are different possible translations of a Latin ablative absolute.

The absolute construction is not wrong, merely stilted and clumsy. In my own editing, I always delete it and make some appropriate substitution.

In summary, let us avoid any passionate devotion to the various forms of the verb *to be*.

OF

In a major university a department head addressed a meeting of his graduate students:

> The present meeting has been occasioned by an acute sense of horror created in me by the recent perusal of the first drafts of a large number of literary ventures submitted by various members of this department.

This quotation comes not from any off-the-cuff remarks, hastily spoken and literally transcribed, but from a published version that had already been revised. The professor had wanted the students to improve the quality of their writing. If the quotation represents the style of the professor, we may indeed wonder just what sort of writing the students had been submitting.

The sentence in question, with 37 words, rests on a single passive verb, *has been occasioned*. Following the verb we find a chain of nine prepositional phrases, among which are interspersed a few modifiers. If we determine what I call the preposition quotient— the ratio of prepositions to total word count—we get 9/37—or virtually 1:4. Almost every fourth word is a preposition.

Prepositions are connecting links that show a relationship between two other terms, that is, between the object of the preposition and the word that the prepositional phrase modifies. Use of too many prepositions creates a disproportion between linking words and the verbs, nouns, and modifiers that bring vigor and life to the sentence. This disproportion can render the sentence ill indeed. A ratio of one preposition to every four words is a bad prognostic sign.

The overuse of prepositions is a severe and extremely common fault. Indeed, if I wanted to offer a single rule for improving the quality of writing, I would unhesitatingly say, Reduce the number of prepositions.

How many prepositions are too many? To this question I can give no clear answer, but I will mention some warning indicators. Long sentences that are not easy to understand and that have only one or two verbs, either copulas or passives, should make you suspect that the sentence has too many prepositions. The real test is, Does elimination of prepositions improve the sentence?

To cut down on prepositions, I suggest several techniques. In pointing to certain constructions that lend themselves to change, I do not mean to imply that those constructions should always be changed. If, however, you want to reduce the number of prepositions, here are a few ways to do so.

1. Delete an entire prepositional phrase as meaningless or unnecessary. "*In order to provide a refuge*" means nothing more than "*To provide* a refuge.*" By deleting *in order* we have eliminated a preposition.

2. Convert a prepositional phrase into a participle. "*In the attempt* to cross the river" can become "*Attempting* to cross the river.*" Sometimes such a conversion can kill off two prepositions in one stroke. "*In the fear of reprisal*, he . . ." can become "*Fearing* reprisal, he. . . .*"

3. Convert a prepositional phrase to an adverb. "Of the six patients treated *by surgery*, three died," becomes "Of the six patients treated *surgically*, three died." Or convert to an adjective: "It is a question *of importance*" becomes "It is an *important* question."

4. Change the passive voice to the active. "The blood volume *was determined by the technician*" becomes "*The technician determined* the blood volume."

34

These are simple ways to get rid of prepositions. Other modes may require extensive change in the sentence structure and cannot be reduced to rules. We may, for example, need to chop one sentence into two, or convert a simple sentence into one that is complex or compound, or provide various transpositions, all depending on the particular example.

Let us now see how we can apply these techniques to some concrete examples. We may start by analyzing this following sentence and trying to improve it.

There had been major changes *in* the presentation related *to* the data accumulated *as* a consequence *of* exhaustive study *of* the results *of* treatment *in* cancers *of* the head and neck, breast, and gynecological tract.

This example fulfills our criteria for excessive prepositions: a long sentence, a single verb in the passive, and considerable obscurity. There are thirty-five words and eight prepositions, with a ratio of just over 1:4.

First let us try to clear up the obscurities. To what does *related* refer? Is the *presentation* related to the data, or are the *changes* related to the data? The latter seems to make more sense, that is, changes (in the presentation) occurred as a result, somehow, of someone studying the accumulated data. Who made the changes? Who studied the data? The sentence, in the passive voice, does not tell us, but we can assume that it was the author of the book.

To begin our revision, we can transfer the passive to the active: "The author made major changes in his presentation." What led him to do so? Presumably he gathered together the results of treatment of the various cases, then made an exhaustive study of these data, and as a result changed his own presentation. If this is correct, how can we express it most clearly?—by eliminating prepositions according to the suggestions given above. For example, "*as* a consequence *of* exhaustive study *of*" becomes "*after* exhaustively studying"; "*of* treatment *in* cancers" becomes "*of* treated cancers." The wording "data accumulated *as* a consequence *of*" is a verbose way of saying "accumulated data," but the sentence loses nothing if we omit this entirely. Putting all these alterations together we have,

> The author made changes *in* his presentation *after* exhaustively studying the results *of* treated cancers *of* the head and neck, breast, and gynecological tract.

Here, then, is a simple sentence of twenty-five words and four prepositions. The revision keeps close to the original but eliminates useless verbiage. If, however, we want to modify the construction, we might say,

> The author changed his presentation after he had exhaustively studied the results *of* treated cancers *of* the head and neck, breast, and gynecological tract.

Now we have a complex sentence rather than a simple one, with twenty-four words altogether, two verbs in the active voice, and only two prepositions. Is not this an improvement?

Here is a truly grim example.

> *From* 1969 *to* 1972, 12 medical centers *throughout* the United States have cooperated *in* a prospective controlled study *of* the effectiveness *of* γ-globulin *in* preventing post-transfusion hepatitis *in* 4,210 patients undergoing pulmonary resection.

This simple sentence, with thirty-four words, has eight prepositions, three preceding and five following the single verb *have cooperated.* Again we have a preposition index of approximately 1:4.

The sentence is perfectly grammatical. It is, perhaps, not unduly obscure, at least on the second reading, but it lacks all the properties of graceful writing. We can improve it by cutting down the number of prepositions, introducing more verbs or verbals, and rearranging the phrases. There are many possible ways of doing this. I suggest the following:

> To determine how effective γ-globulin might be *in* preventing post-transfusion hepatitis, 12 medical centers *throughout* the United States have cooperated *in* a prospective controlled study that utilized 4,210 patients undergoing pulmonary resection *from* 1969 *to* 1972.

We have increased the number of verbs from one to three and made the sentence complex rather than simple. Since this change required additional words to maintain sound grammar, we have actually increased the number of words to thirty-five, but the number of prepositions has diminished to five. The sentence is unequivocally clear; furthermore, it reads smoothly. We have accomplished this by transforming prepositional phrases into verbs or verbals and rearranging the ideas in a more logical order.

Let us study the following sentence, taken from a context that dealt with the relations between the medical profession and the community.

> Increasing the professional morale and the skill *in* management *of* illness resulted *in* a pride and prestige *in* the group that lessened the need *for* community regulation *of* moral behavior and technical skill.

This sentence, whose thirty-three words include six prepositions, rests on two verbs. The clause "that lessened. . ." has, however, an ambiguous reference. What does the clause modify—did the *group* lessen the need or did the *pride and prestige* lessen the need? Obviously the latter, although the sentence as written allows room for doubt. Except for the ambiguous reference the sentence is entirely grammatical and certainly does not shriek for improvement. Let us see, however, if eliminating prepositions will improve the writing.

Suppose we change "*in* management *of* illness" to "*in* managing illness" and also change "resulted *in*" to another verb that says the same thing but does not need a preposition—for example, "*induced*"; and then transpose the phrase "*in* the group." The first part of the sentence will then read, "Increasing the professional morale and the skill *in* managing illness induced *in* the group a pride and prestige that. . . ." The ambiguity is gone and we can now work with the last part of the sentence. We have the awkward phrase "*for* community regulation *of.*" The preposition "*for*" has as its object the noun *regulation,* while *community* is a noun-modifier of *regulation.* We eliminate this undesirable construction by changing the phrase "regulation *of*" not to a participle but to the infinitive *to regulate.* Then *community* is the subject of the infinitive, and *moral behavior* its object. The whole sentence, thus edited, then reads,

> Increasing the professional morale and the skill *in* managing illness induced *in* the group a pride and prestige that lessened the need *for* the community to regulate moral behavior and technical skill.

There are now thirty-two words and two verbs, but the six prepositions have been reduced to three. The reader should decide whether the revision has yielded a better sentence.

A further comparable example,

> Dr. Roe and his coauthors are to be commended *for* bringing together *in* one volume the techniques *for* the performance *of* operations *in* all of the "anatomic specialties" *of* plastic surgery.

This sentence, with its single verb, has thirty-one words and seven prepositions. Improvement is easy. We compress *are to be commended* into the adverb *commendably,* but this leaves us without any verb at all. We get the verb back by changing the phrase *bringing together* into the verb form, *have brought together.* We reduce "techniques *for* the performance *of* operations" to the simple *op-*

erative techniques. In the phrase *"in* all *of* the 'anatomic specialties'" the *of* is totally redundant and should be omitted. The entire sentence then reads,

> Commendably, Dr. Roe and his coauthors have brought together in one volume the operative techniques *in* all the "anatomic specialties" *of* plastic surgery.

There are now twenty-three words, one active verb, and only three prepositions.

Here is a sentence that I would characterize as truly foggy.

> Since biotransformation may result *in* destruction *of* the biologically active form *of* a chemical or formation *of* a more toxic product, it is apparent that the presence or absence *of* such mechanisms *within* members *of* a species will effectively alter the concentration *of* the parent chemical *in* the biological specimen.

The forty words in this sentence include nine prepositions and the three verbs *may result, is,* and *will alter.*

What is the author trying to tell us? I believe the message is that biotransformation can alter the concentration of chemicals in biological specimens; and the sentence also tells us the reasons why this is so. We can readily improve this. We can change the phrase *"in* destruction *of"* to *destroy.* Thus, instead of "Biotransformation may result *in* the destruction *of.* . . ." we will have "Biotransformation may destroy. . . ." We can similarly change "formation *of* a more toxic product" into "form a more toxic product." However, since we already have the word *form* as a noun, we should not use the same word as a verb but should seek some synonym, such as *yield*—"[Biotransformation may] yield a more toxic product." Then, to improve the sentence, we can delete without loss the words "it is apparent that the presence or absence of such mechanisms within members of the species," which merely cloud the sense without contributing anything. Since this deletion also eliminates both the grammatical subject and the main verb, we can make "biotransformation" the grammatical subject of the sentence and use *"will alter"* as the main verb. We then have,

> Biotransformation, which may destroy the biologically active form of a chemical or yield a more toxic product, will effectively alter the concentration *of* the parent chemical *in* the biological specimen.

We now have only thirty words, three verbs (*may destroy*, [*may*] *yield*, and *will alter*), and only three prepositions.

I have a rule of thumb that no simple sentence should have more than four prepositions, and not more than three prepositional phrases consecutively. If there are more than four altogether, or more than three in sequence, I eliminate at least one. The following example, to illustrate this point, has the single verb *is* and five prepositions, four of them in a chain.

> The purpose *of* Dr. Roe's book is the scrutiny *of* the events attributed *to* the activities *of* the agents *of* various foreign governments.

By this time the words "is the scrutiny *of*" should irritate the reader and call loudly for simple relief. We eliminate the *is* and change *scrutiny* to a verb. *Scrutinize* sounds rather precious and might better be replaced by *examines,* or even *examines carefully* (to get the full flavor of *scrutiny*). What, then, do we do with *the purpose of?* Simply omit it. The sentence would then read,

> Dr. Roe's book examines carefully the events attributed *to* the activities *of* the agents *of* various foreign governments.

If the reader feels strongly about retaining some sense of "purpose," he can say, "In this book, Dr. Roe wants to examine. . . ." I personally would not say this but I would not argue with those who might prefer it.

Ordinarily, when we diagnose sentences as having too many prepositions, we will want to institute appropriate changes and yet preserve the original sense. But from time to time we will come across sentences like this.

> *For* this reason an awareness had developed *in* recent years that research design directed *toward* an evaluation *of* the relative contributions made *by* different types *of* basic processes *to* the functional losses characteristic *of* age is the "sine qua non" of the rapid development of biological understanding *of* the aging phenomenon.

This sentence has fifty words, two verbs, and eleven prepositions. Obviously too many. But how can we remedy this? Under ordinary circumstances we would first try to analyze the meaning. But here I find myself utterly baffled, for I simply cannot understand what the author is trying to say. Every once in a while, as I go back repeatedly to this sentence, I think I may have grasped at least part of the meaning, but I cannot be sure. In a case like this I would simply discard the whole sentence. And if there were many sentences like it, I would discard the entire manuscript.

AND

Conjunctions, as the name indicates, join together two or more terms, whether these be words, phrases, or whole clauses. Conjunctions are of two sorts. Especially important for this chapter is the class called coordinating—*and, but, or.* The second type we call subordinating—*if, as, when, because.* Let us first consider the coordinating conjunctions.

These join together two terms of equal standing, like two horses yoked together in parallel. The compounding or joining can take place at various grammatical levels. We can have a compound sentence, in which two or more independent clauses are joined together by a coordinating conjunction: "John went home *and* Mary followed." We can have a simple sentence containing a compound subject and a single verb: "Jack *and* Jill went up the hill"; or a single subject with a compound verb: "Jack fell down *and* broke his crown." A verb may have a compound object: "He distributed praise *and* blame"; and so too may a preposition: "He spoke kindly to his nephews *and* nieces." We can have a conjunction of prepositional phrases—two phrases in parallel construction,

joined by *and*: "He walked across the hall *and* into the bedroom."
"Across the hall" is a prepositional phrase and so is "into the
bedroom." They both modify the verb "walked," while the *and*
shows their togetherness. We can place adjectives, adverbs, or
gerundives into a similar relationship: "The night was calm *and*
peaceful." "He spoke clearly *and* distinctly." "Getting *and* spending
we lay waste our powers." In all these examples the terms joined
by *and* are grammatically coordinate.

Coordinating conjunctions, then, join terms that are equals—
neither limits the other in a grammatical sense. The terms thus
joined may be complete sentences or parts of sentences— nouns,
verbs, adjectives, adverbs, prepositional phrases, gerunds, and
gerundives—indeed, any grammatical element that permits a
junction.

Subordinating conjunctions are rather different. Instead of
equality they show inequality, a relationship of dependence and of
limitation. Let us study a simple example.

I will go *if* it does not rain.

This consists of a main clause, "I will go," independent and capable
of standing alone but limited by a second clause, "*if* it does not
rain." Since this clause cannot stand by itself, we call it dependent.
It must attach to something else, and in so doing it alters the
meaning of the clause to which it is attached. "I will go" means
one thing; "I will go *if* it does not rain" means something quite
different.

The meaning of the sentence will vary according to the conjunction.

I will go *if* it rains.
I will go *after* it rains.
I will go *because* it rains.

All have different meanings, but only the conjunction has
changed.

We identify sentences according to kinds of conjunctions. A
sentence is compound when it has two or more independent clauses

joined by a coordinating conjunction. A complex sentence has a main clause and at least one subordinate clause (but it may have more than one). We call a sentence compound-complex when it has at least two independent clauses, conjoined, and at least one dependent clause.

In this section, concerned chiefly with parallelism, I use *and* as the prototype for all coordinating conjunctions. Whatever I say about *and* applies equally well to the others. I will not discuss the problems of complex sentences.

And should connect terms that are grammatically similar, that is, that exhibit a parallel construction. When parallelism exists, the conjunction of terms is grammatically sound (even though it may be clumsy). When there is no parallelism, the result can lead to varying degrees of awkwardness and confusion, even to massive bafflement.

Young children often tend to string their thoughts together with a succession of *ands*, thus creating a single interminable sentence whose separate components have lost touch with each other. We can imagine a child speaking thus:

> My mother told me to go to the store on my way to school *and* so I dressed quickly *and* ate my breakfast *and* after breakfast I started to school *and* after walking two blocks I forgot what I was supposed to get *and* so I had to go home *and* I asked her again *and* she was mad at me.

This sentence could go on indefinitely and yet remain grammatically correct (or, let us say, not incorrect). Every word, phrase, and clause will parse without confusion, yet it is hardly graceful. We should improve it markedly if we lysed a few of the *ands* and thus dissolved some of the bonds that tie the clauses together. Yet this behemoth sentence, however ungainly, does have the virtue of parallelism.

I will give several examples of faulty usage, some glaringly obvious, others more subtle. The reader should acquire a sensitivity, so that wrong constructions will act as an irritant and provoke acute discomfort. At first he may not be able to pinpoint the fault or know how to correct it. But if he realizes that something is wrong and tries to analyze the grammar to identify the precise error, then correction should be relatively easy.

My first example comes from an advertisement, printed in three lines, with a broad space between the second and third. The ellipsis dots are part of the original advertisement.

For your many patients
who should avoid aspirin . . .

and for when they catch colds.

What does the *and* connect? Not the two naked prepositions *for*, but rather the two prepositional phrases. In judging parallelism we must consider the total *terms* that are united. In this instance each term is a phrase introduced by the preposition *for*, but the two individual phrases do not have a parallel structure. "For your many patients" is quite clear. The preposition governs an object, the noun *patients*. The second *for*, however, is followed not by a noun object but by a clause, "when they catch colds." "For your many patients" and "for when they catch colds" are discordant, and to connect them by *and* is grating indeed.

What is the ad really trying to say? Presumably, that the drug is useful for two classes of patients—those who should avoid aspirin and those who have caught cold. These two thoughts are not coordinate. They demand separate sentences. In this instance, I merely point out the fault. I will not try to correct it.

Here is a confusing sentence whose faults are due to lack of parallelism.

The first part of the book describes operations on the adrenal gland, for tumors that produce endocrinologic changes, *and* also to remove the gland for patients with metastases from breast carcinoma.

In this clumsy sentence the verb *describes* has as its object the noun *operations*, and the writer is distinguishing two different types of surgery: "operations . . . for tumors" and "[operations] to remove the gland." In this original example the *and* tries to join a prepositional phrase, *for tumors*, and an infinitive, *to remove*. These are not parallel. To make the sentence grammatical we should have either two prepositional phrases or two infinitives. It seems easier to have two infinitives. Thus,

> The first part of the book describes operations on the adrenal gland, to remove tumors that produce endocrinologic changes, *and* to take out the gland in patients with metastases from breast carcinoma.

The sentence, although still nothing to be proud of, is at least grammatical.

Another example,

> He had fallen in love with *and* married a girl who had worked in a department store.

At first glance we might think that the *and* connected the two verbs, but this is not correct. If we break the sentence down into its components, we find "He had fallen in love with a girl who. . . ." and "[he] married a girl who. . . ." The verb *had fallen*, intransitive, does not take an object, and to complete the sense a prepositional phrase is added; however, *married* is a transitive verb with the object *girl*. In this example, the single noun, *girl*, is performing two separate grammatical functions—the object of the preposition *with* and the object of the verb *married*. We can rectify the fault by having separate objects for the preposition and for the verb.

> He had fallen in love with a girl who worked in a department store *and* had married her.

"He had fallen in love. . . ." and "[he] had married her" are now grammatically parallel and may appropriately be connected by *and*.

Here is a comparable example.

> Doctors Doe and Roe have written an excellent account of the chemistry of collagen which probably far surpasses *and* is unlike any other treatise on the subject.

If we analyze what this means, we find three separate concepts: The two doctors have written an excellent account; this account surpasses any other on the subject; and this account is unlike any other on the subject. The *and*, in the sentence as given, connects the last two thoughts. But grammatically we run into difficulties, for the two clauses have in common the word *treatise*, and this word has a different construction in each clause. *Surpass* is a transitive verb and properly takes an object, namely, *treatise*. However, *is* is a copula that takes not an object but a complement— in this case the phrase "unlike any other treatise." Here, *treatise* is the object of the preposition *unlike*. In the sentence as given the single word *treatise* thus serves as object of both a verb and a preposition, a lack of parallelism created by the misuse of *and*.

We might try a simple remedy by merely deleting the term "*and* is unlike."

> Doctors Doe and Roe have written an excellent account of the chemistry of collagen, which probably far surpasses any other treatise on the subject.

But this revision has a possible ambiguity. What is the reference of the pronoun *which*? Is it *collegen* or *chemistry* or *account*? We can eliminate the ambiguity by recasting the sentence into a still better form.

> In their excellent account of the chemical aspects of collagen, Doctors Doe and Roe have written a treatise which probably far surpasses any other on the subject.

When the misuse of *and* gets us into trouble, we can often rescue the sentence by recasting it to eliminate the *and*.

The next example, using the conjunction *and* three times, is more difficult. There is a further complication from the use of a noun-modifier. The quotation comes from a book review, in which the reviewer discusses the purpose of the authors.

The text is written for the physician involved with birth control services *and* to help train clinicians *and* staff in IUD insertion, removal, *and* patient management. [*IUD stands for "intrauterine device."*]

Let us start by analyzing the fault attending the first *and*. It connects two thoughts: "the text is written for the physician involved with birth control services" and "[the text is written] to help train clinicians. . . ." The *and* joins two nonparallel terms, the prepositional phrase "for the physician" and the infinitive "to help." The remedy can take one of three forms: make both terms prepositional phrases, make them both infinitives, or get rid of one of them and thus eliminate the need for parallelism. In the present instance the last course seems best. We can say,

The text, written for the physician involved with birth control services, will help to train clinicians. . . .

In the original sentence, the second *and* is correctly used. It joins *clinicians* and *staff*, terms entirely correlative.

The third *and* involves severe confusion. There are three terms, *insertion, removal,* and *patient management.* The original sentence would imply that these three are parallel, whereas actually they are not. We realize this if we consider the modifier *IUD.* If parallelism existed, IUD would modify all three nouns equally. But clearly, it does nothing of the sort. *IUD insertion* and *IUD removal* make good sense. But *IUD patient management* does not. *Insertion* and *removal* revolve around one thought, while *management* refers to a different thought. The reviewer wants to say that the book will help to train clinicians in IUD insertion; that it will help train clinicians in IUD removal; and that it will help train clinicians in patient management. But that is not what the sentence actually says.

We can eliminate the confusion if we eliminate the noun-modifier in favor of a prepositional phrase. We solve the problem if we say that the book will "train clinicians in insertion and removal of intrauterine devices, and in patient management." Inserting the extra *in* shows that the phrases *in insertion* and *in management* are parallel, both modifying the verb *train*. Hence, the phrases are properly connected by the conjunction *and*. The corrected sentence would then read,

> The text, written for physicians involved with birth control services, will help [to] train clinicians and staff in the insertion and removal of the IUD, and in patient management.

This is far from elegant, but it is at least grammatical.

The misuse of *and* can produce monstrosities that almost defy repair. Here is a sentence whose context has to do with the care of emotionally disturbed patients.

> Physicians reported that more than half of the emotionally disturbed patients were as easy to work with, required no more time to treat, and showed as good or better improvement than other patients.

This sentence offers a series of comparisons between patients that are emotionally disturbed and those that are not. All the comparisons lead to the clause "than other patients [with a verb understood]." But clearly, some of the comparisons require the conjunction *as*, while others require *than*. Some require the verb *were*, understood; others the verb *did*, understood. Thus, we should say,

> as easy to work with *as* other patients [were]
> required no more time *than* other patients [did]
> showed as good improvement [ugh!] *as* other patients [did]
> showed better improvement [ugh!] *than* other patients [did]

The original sentence, by compressing a lot of quite different constructions and running them together in reckless fashion, has produced a grammatical disaster quite hopeless to repair. The sentence must be completely recast with entirely different constructions. I would suggest the following:

> Physicians reported that more than half the emotionally disturbed patients responded just as quickly to treatment as did the others, *and* improved at least as rapidly.

This is entirely grammatical. The *and* connects the strictly coordinate verbs *responded* and *improved*. However, the reader may want to recast in a different fashion.

Many times we have sentences that are grammatical and really do exhibit parallelism but are awkward or even utterly absurd. Here is an example of the latter category.

Forty percent of all women seeking abortions were married to *and* impregnated by their husbands, according to Dr. Doe.

The noun *husbands* serves as the object of two different prepositions, *to* and *by*. The conjunction *and*, however, does not connect the prepositions but rather the two verbs, each with its modifying prepositional phrase. Moreover, the sentence is absurdly redundant, for to be married means to have a husband, and it is not possible for a woman to be married to anyone other than her husband. We rescue the sentence by deleting the words *married to and*, with this result.

Forty percent of all women seeking abortions were impregnated by their husbands, according to Dr. Doe.

Here is a further example of severe awkwardness resulting from faulty usage. The context has to do with certain research reports.

Many of the contributions deal with gastrointestinal epithelium because of the ease with which it can be studied in the laboratory *and* also its inherently high replication rate.

What does the *and* connect? The sentence has three separate thoughts: the contributions deal with gastrointestinal epithelium, this epithelium can be easily studied in the laboratory, and this epithelium has a high replication rate. The thoughts are causally related: because there is a high replication rate, the epithelium is easily studied, and because it is easily studied, there are many contributions on the subject. In the original sentence the *and* connects two nouns, *ease* and *rate*, both objects of the same preposition *of*—once expressed and once understood: "because *of* the ease"and "[because *of* the] inherently high replication rate." But these two objects are widely separated by intervening verbiage.

The sentence would be improved if, instead of using two widely separated nouns as the objects of a single preposition, we substituted verbs. Furthermore, we could place the thoughts in a more logical order to indicate better the causal relationship. I suggest this revision.

> Many of the contributions deal with gastrointestinal epithelium because it has an inherently high replication rate *and* can be readily studied in the laboratory.

The subordinate clause introduced by *because* has a single subject, *it*, and a compound verb, *has* and *can be studied*, joined by *and*. We have eliminated useless words and made the sentence more compact and more logical.

Here is another, somewhat comparable, example. The context concerns the curriculum in a medical school.

> The number of hours allocated to *and* the form of these courses varied widely.

The *and* would seem to connect *allocated to* and *form of*, but grammatically this is not the case. The *and* actually connects the two nouns, *number* and *form*. The number of hours varied widely and the form of the courses varied widely. Thus the one verb has a compound subject *number and form*. But then the author has introduced some modifiers. *Number* is modified by the phrase *of hours*, while *hours* is modified by the participle *allocated*; *allocated* is modified by the phrase *to these courses*. The other half of the subject, *form*, is modified by the phrase *of these courses*. The one noun *courses* serves as object in two different prepositional phrases that are not parallel—one phrase modifies a participle and thus is adverbial in nature, the other modifies a noun and is adjectival.

To straighten out the difficulty I suggest two possibilities. First, retain the compound subject and the single verb, but give each prepositional phrase a separate object. A rendition grammatically correct but dreadfully clumsy would be,

> The number of hours allocated to these courses and the form of the courses varied widely.

Some minor changes would slightly improve the flow but retain the same format.

> The form of these courses *and* the number of hours allocated to them varied widely.

However, this would be improved if, instead of being a simple sentence with a compound subject, it was a compound sentence.

> The number of hours allocated to the courses varied widely *and* so did their form [vary widely, understood].

The *and* now connects two independent and coordinate clauses. In contrast, I offer this example.

> The information was passed along to *and* shared by the hospital staff.

This sentence has a single subject, *information*, and a compound verb, each part of which has its modifiers. The information, we learn, was passed along to the hospital staff, and the same information was shared by the hospital staff. We note that the two prepositional phrases, modifying separate verbs, nevertheless have a single object, *staff*. However, each phrase is adverbial in character, and the two are strictly parallel.

In this sentence, what does the *and* connect? Not the verb

forms, not the prepositional phrases, but the two halves of the compound predicate. These halves, strictly coordinate, exhibit parallelism; the *and* is appropriately used. However, although the sentence is grammatical, I consider it clumsy and undesirable. I would revise the structure so that two prepositions do not govern the same object. I believe the sentence is much more pleasing if we change the construction and say,

> The hospital staff shared the information that had been passed along to them.

This gives a complex sentence with a subordinate clause, instead of a simple sentence with a dual predicate. The *and* has disappeared. However, the original format was not wrong, and those who like it better than my version are welcome to their preference. Some people like gooseberries, others don't.

Regardless of preference in any individual case, I would recommend a general rule in regard to *and*: Every time you use it, ask yourself the question, What does it connect? If you cannot give an instant and clear answer, make some changes in your constructions.

VERY

I use the adverb *very* to exemplify the general class of modifiers. A modifier limits the meaning of some other term. The most common modifiers are adjectives, which modify nouns; and adverbs, which modify verbs, adjectives, and other adverbs. Take a random noun—say, *boy.* It indicates any male child without distinction; add an adjective, like *tall,* and you immediately create a limit. Tom, Dick, and Harry are all boys, but only Tom is tall.

Adjectives have a descriptive function. We can build up a picture by piling one adjective on top of another—one boy is tall, strong, handsome, and generous; another is tall, spindly, feeble, and spiteful. These various adjectives do not react on each other but all modify the noun *boy.* Adverbs, however, among their other functions, can modify adjectives and limit their meaning. *Very, slightly, exceedingly,* and *surprisingly* will each change the meaning of the adjective in a different way. "The boy is very tall" conveys a picture quite different from "The boy is surprisingly tall."

Adverbs modify verbs: "He walked quickly" or "He walked slowly." Furthermore, some adverbs can also modify other adverbs. "He walked surprisingly quickly" is not at all the same as "He walked quickly."

The class of modifiers also includes prepositional phrases which may limit the meaning of either nouns or verbs. "The girl with the blonde hair" contains an adjectival phrase. This can itself contain an adverbial modifier: "The girl with the artificially blonde hair." There are also adverbial phrases: "He cried out in a loud voice." Sometimes such a phrase may be replaced by a simpler modifier that conveys the same limitation: "He cried out loudly." The adverb *loudly* is more or less the equivalent of the adverbial phrase "in a loud voice."

As we saw in the discussion of conjunctions, subordinate clauses also exert a modifying or limiting function. In the complex sentence "The boy is tall when he stands up straight," the subordinate clause "when he stands up straight" limits the meaning of the main clause "the boy is tall." In this section I will discuss a few problems that involve modifiers but will not consider prepositional phrases and limiting clauses.

Modifiers, then, qualify and limit the terms to which they apply. Badly used, they can render writing flabby. It is easy to make a general rule, "Avoid excessive use of adjectives (or adverbs)," but such a rule has singularly little value. How much is too much? How many adjectives should a sentence have? Although we cannot answer such questions, we can identify certain contexts that do have too many modifiers (and sometimes even one modifier is too many).

Let us start with the word *very*, which provides the heading for this section. This word derives, ultimately, from the Latin *verus*, true; and some sense of true or truth attaches to the various meanings. *Very* is both an adjective—"the *very* end," "the *very* idea"—and an adverb that modifies an adjective (to indicate a higher stage or degree). We may call it an intensifier. "A beautiful picture" has one meaning; "a *very* beautiful picture" indicates a higher grade of beauty.

Beautiful is an adjective so hackneyed that it has lost all force and really indicates little more than mild to moderate approval. When an adjective becomes merely vapid instead of expressive, we may try to restore some of its lost vigor by adding *very*. If the mind no longer reacts to a verbal stimulus, the adverb *very* tries to increase that stimulus. However, since the mind will soon adapt to that added stimulus, then further intensification will be necessary if we want to attract attention. In movie advertisements each new film may carry an epithet more extravagant than its predecessor. *Very* is far too pale. If one picture is *stupendous,* the next will be *colossal,* and the next *supercolossal.* But such extravagance carries the seeds of its own destruction. A few years ago this story was making the rounds: A Hollywood producer described to a friend the latest picture from his studio. "It is marvelous, tremendous, breathtaking, colossal—why, it might even be *good.*"

The adverb *very* has become emasculated through overuse. I would make this suggestion: Every time you have the impulse to write *very,* restrain the impulse and see whether the omission would entail any real loss of meaning. At first you will almost certainly say, Yes, something *is* lost. But I predict that if you persevere, you will gradually agree that any loss is negligible. *Very* is one of the words that contributes to flabby writing.

Adjectives, when overused and tired, contribute but little and may even detract. This is especially noticeable when virtually every noun is modified by an overworked adjective. Take, for example, the following advertisement.

> The world-*famous* Jumbo cruise offers an *unusual* opportunity to enjoy a *rare* close-up view of the *magnificent* estates and *lavish tropical* gardens which line the *secluded private* islands and *beautiful* waterways of Doolittle Beach. Here you will have the *rare* opportunity of visiting the *magnificent formal* gardens, studded with *sparkling* fountains, *crystal* pools, *beautiful* statuary and *sculptured* colonnades.

Almost every noun has its adjective, and the net result is tiresome and dull.

Overloading with adjectives was at one time perfectly acceptable. Indeed, adjectives, if forceful, may provide considerable impact. Here is one example, written in 1849, that described the social environment in the slums where a cholera epidemic flourished.

It is in a nation's dens of poverty, where *unrequiting* toil pines for its *daily* food, where nakedness shivers in the *wintry* air, where the *miserable* victims of *unjust* conditions of society hive together in *damp* cellars and *unhealthy* garrets, where the *blessed* air of Heaven is tainted by *unventilated* streets and *dark* and *obscure* alleys, where *pure* water is a luxury. . . .

To the modern ear these words sound stilted. The quotation is not without force, but the effectiveness derives as much from a few striking verbs—*pine, shiver,* and *hive*—as from the overabundant adjectives.

Here is a further example from a little-read Victorian novel, *Coningsby,* by Disraeli. He was writing about youthful leaders in politics who might in time lose their idealism.

[Will] their enthusiasm evaporate before *hollow-hearted* ridicule, their *generous* impulses yield with a *vulgar* catastrophe to the *tawdry* temptation of a *low* ambition? Will their *skilled* intelligence subside into being the *adroit* tool of a *corrupt* party?

And the rhetoric goes on and on. Many of the adjectives, individually, are forceful and by no means hackneyed, but the combination of adjective and noun, adjective and noun, in monotonous sequence, now seems both pompous and wearing.

On the other hand a transposition of modifiers may restore freshness and vigor when the adjectives themselves are trite. The same author describes a reunion of old schoolmates.

And yet there is perhaps no occasion when the heart is more *open,* the brain more *quick,* the memory more *rich* and *happy,* or the tongue more *prompt* and *eloquent,* than when two school-friends meet.

We can appreciate the effectiveness if we reverse the position of adjectives and nouns into the more usual order.

no occasion when there is a more open heart, a more quick brain, a more rich and happy memory, or a more prompt and eloquent tongue.

This is dull, whereas the original version had some sparkle and rhythm. The placing of the adjective after the noun instead of before it is often a most helpful technique.

Overloading with adjectives is a fault common in medical writing. Here is a simple example from a book review.

The *excellent* chapters on *legal* principles contain warnings about *mandatory* testing, which appear in *muted* form in the *terse* recommendation section but could bear *added* emphasis.

This passage contains eight nouns, of which one, *recommendation*, serves as a modifier, the so-called noun-modifier. Of the remaining seven nouns, six are preceded by adjectives. Only *warnings* remains unmodified. Yet despite the overload of adjectives, the sentence has an important merit: Of the twenty-six words, three are verbs. These tend to mask the numerous adjectives, so that they do not seem overly intrusive. Compare it with the following sentence, concerned with the lungs in emphysema.

Specimens containing *progressive* stages of *minimal* to moderately *advanced, subclinical, localized* but pathologically *typical, obstructive pulmonary* emphysema were utilized for the study of *early* and *developing bronchiolar* and *respiratory* tissue lesions.

Here are thirty-one words, resting on a single verb. Apart from the subject, *specimens*, there are four nouns functioning as such (*tissue* is a noun-modifier and therefore functions as an adjective) and twelve adjectives, including the gerundive, or verbal adjective. In addition, two adverbs modify the adjectives, so that altogether there are fourteen modifiers (fifteen, if we include "tissue") bearing down on four nouns, which in turn rest on a single verb. Obviously the sentence has excessive modifiers.

Here is another instructive example.

This *fluent,* highly *readable first English* translation of John Doe's *famous* monograph will be of *special* interest to those interested in the *philosophical* aspects of sociology.

Preceding the noun *translation,* we have four adjectives and an adverb, five modifiers in all, while of the remaining four nouns three have single modifiers.

This reminds us of the Germanic constructions which often encourage long strings of modifiers preceding a noun. Here, for example, is a literal translation from the German.

. . . otherwise the on-the-spit grilled, in-olive-oil-immersed, with pepper-and-salt-thyme-and-mustard-seasoned, and with brown-butter-poured-over, extra-fine lamb kidneys. . . .

But good or at least acceptable German usage does not make good or acceptable English.

Not all authors are sensitive to the differences between German and English. What, for example, can we make of this excerpt.

The average resting and after arginine hydrochloride infusion plasma growth hormone concentration of relatively coronary-prone subjects. . . .

In fairness to the authors we must realize that this comes from a synopsis-abstract, in which the number of words was strictly limited. The authors tried to crowd as much information as possible into a limited number of words. But merely compacting a series of words, without regard to style, produces not a communication of thought but only an indigestible lump.

Some modifiers are forceful. We think of them as possessing vigor; they produce a powerful effect; they call to mind unusual imagery, create associations that lend richness and that fit into a pattern. However, when a modifier becomes trite it loses its force, produces no effect, and even detracts. Masters of prose style avoid piling up commonplace terms which communicate nothing except a sense of intellectual poverty. Let me give an example of superb use of modifiers. Carlyle is describing his thoughts of death.

> And yet, strangely enough, I lived in a *continual, indefinite, pining* fear; *tremulous, pusillanimous, apprehensive* of I knew not what: it seemed as if *all* things in the Heavens above and the Earth beneath would hurt me; as if the Heavens and the Earth were but *boundless* jaws of a *devouring* monster, wherein I, *palpitating*, waited to be devoured.

The modifiers are of two sorts, adjectives and gerundives (or verbal adjectives). The latter, like *pining, devouring,* and *palpitating*, convey the force of their verbs, thus adding an especial vigor. Many of the adjectives precede the words they modify, many others follow. This shift in position prevents the monotony we will see in the next example. Notice that the modifiers have more color and force than do the verbs. The verbs *lived, knew, seemed, hurt, were,* and *waited* are all precise enough, but they do not convey any special imagery. In this sentence the verbs provide the framework that carries the modifiers.

Let us go from a master stylist to an expert in bureaucratic gobbledygook.

> It is a *virtual* certainty that the *spatial* pattern of a city in a *free-enterprise* society is the *collective* result of a large number of *separate business* and *household location* decisions and *transportation* choices.

In this quotation I have placed in italics the modifiers to which I want to call attention. These include adjectives and also nouns, the so-called noun-modifiers. There are no gerundives to lend the force that inheres in verbs. Furthermore, all the modifiers precede nouns. Indeed, if we disregard the noun-modifiers (which are functioning as adjectives) then *city* is the only noun that does not have a modifier preceding it. The prose is lifeless and depressing. Of course, the abuse of modifiers is only one of the faults here. Others include the dispensable clause "It is a virtual certainty that" and, when that is eliminated, the excessive weight that rests on the single verb *is.*

We can digress for a moment and consider the vexing problem of noun-modifiers. In the example quoted the author talks about *free-enterprise society.* This is a not uncommon usage and perhaps is even preferable to the rather clumsy *society devoted to free enterprise.* But we cannot be so tolerant of *business location decisions, hosuehold location decisions,* and *transportation choices.* A single noun-modifier in a sentence might be tolerable, but a series of them is disastrous, especially when two nouns join to modify a third.

Some purists insist that nouns should never serve as modifiers, but this ignores established custom. We constasntly speak of heart disease, science fiction, and virus titers. To be sure, we might say disease of the heart, or titers of the virus, or (with marked distortion) scientific fiction, but these would sound stilted. We should also note that a person who studies law is a law student and not a legal student, even though a person who studies medicine is a medical student and not a medicine student.

Noun-modifiers do have a definite, limited place, established by usage, but the limitations are too often transgressed. Take for example,

Those who address the issue of drug abuse treatment evaluation. . . .

Here we have four nouns in a row, three of them serving to modify the fourth. In this monstrosity there is a hidden difficulty, namely, a tautology. If we leave out the noun-modifiers, we see that the quotation concerns "those who address the issue of evaluation." But this is only a long-winded way of saying "those who evaluate," or even "those who want to evaluate." If we get rid of the useless words, we could readily say,

Those who evaluate the treatment of drug abuse. . . .

This, I believe, is what the author really wanted to say. But, as I emphasize in another chapter, an author usually does not know what he really wants to say until after he has said it clumsily two or three times; and if he should then recognize that his exposition is thoroughly bad, he may be able to cleave to the essence and express his message more gracefully.

I suggest that nouns acting as modifiers should be followed by a hyphen, to indicate a unity-in-duality. We are so accustomed to *heart disease* that a hyphen seems unnecessary. But the hyphen removes the first noun from the category of modifier and makes a single compound noun. *Heart-disease* is one noun. In *heart disease* we have two nouns, the first of which is a modifier. However, as a realist I do not really expect the suggestion of hyphenation to take root and prosper.

We must be careful about chains of modifiers, even when they are legitimate adjectives. Careless writers often will run together a series of adjectives, some appropriate and others quite inappropriate. Here is a sentence that plays fast and loose with modifiers. A critic was describing a dance recital.

These *limber smart understated* yet *joyous* dancers rival what I have seen any *seasoned major arts* institution achieve on a London stage.

Dancers may indeed be limber, smart, and joyous, but what does *understated dancer* mean? Presumably the writer had in mind that the dancers did not exaggerate their activities but exhibited restraint and other comparable qualities. But then only the dancing was understated, not the dancers. The rest of the quoted sentence is indeed clumsy, and we would have great difficulty if we wanted to figure out exactly what the dancers are rivaling, but this is a problem distinct from the misuse of modifiers.

IT

It is a pronoun. There are many kinds of pronouns—personal, relative, possessive, interrogative. Each refers to an antecedent, ordinarily a noun (or pronoun) called a *referent.* In the use of pronouns one great source of confusion lies in faulty or unclear reference—the reader is not sure of the antecedent. This difficulty, especially severe with *it,* also affects other pronouns.

In one usage *it* is correlative with *he* and *she*—personal pronouns that distinguish gender. *He* refers to a specific masculine noun, *she* to a feminine noun, and *it* to one that is neuter. In some languages there are only two genders, so that all nouns are either masculine or feminine, while other languages, like German or English, have three. But in English the great majority of common nouns are neuter. If we want to refer to such diverse entities as *book, kidney, gravitation, truth,* the appropriate pronoun is *it* in each instance.

In a second usage *it* has a more indefinite reference. Suppose we say, "It is going to rain." Grammatically, a verb requires a subject. In this example *it* is called the *anticipatory* subject, but the intended subject is really the phrase *going to rain. It* "anticipates" this phrase, thus serving a grammatical function made necessary by the peculiarities of English. We see comparable functions in the sentence "It is apparent that he is sick." *It* refers to a deferred subject, namely, the whole clause "that he is sick." This clause is the real subject, and *it* is only anticipatory.

Much of this usage stems from Latin constructions with their impersonal verbs, where the subject, an integral part of the verb form, is not represented by any separate word. Verbs of this character, translated into English, may have a separate subject. For example, *oportet,* "it is proper" (or "appropriate"); *licet,* "it is allowed" (or, to use a different impersonal construction in translation, "one may"); *constat,* "it is well known." To indicate *what* is apparent, or permissible, or well known, the Latin might use a clause in the subjunctive; or, more commonly, have an infinitive construction, whose subject would be in the accusative case. We

61

can get the flavor of this if we think of the English, "It is proper to wear sport clothes," "It is proper for me to wear sport clothes," or "It is proper that I wear sport clothes." The Latin does not need the introductory *it*.

However, there are Latin constructions closer to the English; such as *opus est*, "there is a need" (or "it is necessary"). Here, too, the Latin generally uses the infinitive construction to tell us what is necessary. We see this in the English, "It is necessary to hurry," "There is need to hurry," or more idiomatically, "We must hurry."

In these examples the *it* has a relatively diffuse reference, namely, an entire phrase or clause. For convenience I will call this the indefinite usage, which I would contrast with the highly specific reference wherein the *it* stands for a particular and clearly identified noun. Thus, in the sentences, "Where is my book? Is it on the table?", *it* is a pronoun of unambiguous and specific reference.

Unfortunately, many authors confuse these two, and sprinkle their sentences with numerous *its* so that the reader loses all track of the intended reference. The single word *it* is forced to do double duty in totally different contexts, sometimes definite, sometimes indefinite. Here is an example.

> *It* is a natural impulse, when the manuscript is completed, to put *it* in an envelope and mail *it* to the editor.

In this sentence the word *it* occurs three times, once as an anticipatory subject and twice as a pronoun referring to specific nouns. But which noun? and How do you know? In the example quoted, the second *it* clearly refers to the *manuscript*, but what does the last *it* refer to, *manuscript* or *envelope*? In this instance the exact reference makes little difference, since the manuscript is in the envelope and if you mail one you are automatically mailing the other. But if we want to be precise, we find scope for confusion.

While there is no rigid grammatical rule, the general tendency is to refer the pronoun to the preceding noun of appropriate gender and number. A singular pronoun will not refer to a plural noun nor the neuter *it* to a feminine noun. But once we have said that, there is a certain amount of leeway. The grammar books tell us that an antecedent should be reasonably close to the pronoun; that no other likely or plausible antecedent should intervene; and, if the antecedent and pronoun are not immediately close together, that the antecedent should be the important word in its context. All this allows considerable possibility of confusion. The reference should always be sufficiently close that the reader need not stop to inquire what the author really means.

Let me give a few further instances. In this example, the subject of discourse is hypertension.

Any proposed concept needs constant testing and revision. *It* is only in this way that *it* can be useful.

The first *it* represents an anticipatory construction, but the second is a relative pronoun whose reference is not immediately apparent. When we look carefully, we see that the second *it* refers to *concept* in the preceding sentence. Intervening between the intended referent and the *it* are nouns *testing, revision,* and *way.* To find the reference, the reader must skip over these and go back to a noun far removed from the pronoun.

A little care would remove the confusion and also make the sentence much more graceful. Thus, the anticipatory *it* could be deleted with positive gain. The second sentence would then read, "Only in this way can *it* be useful." But even this is not really clear, for the ambiguous reference of the second *it* still remains. The simplest mode of correction is to recast the two sentences and combine them.

Any proposed concept needs constant testing and revision, which alone can make *it* useful.

The *which* refers unambiguously to *testing and revision,* and the *it* then has a clear track to its referent *concept.* One road to greater clarity is to obey an *ad hoc* rule: Do not have more than one *it* in any single sentence.

Here is another example. The context discusses a particular television program.

> *It* was called *Forum,* and in a rather clumsy way, *it* did attempt to give the public a platform from which *it* could criticize the programs that were being inflicted on *it.* *It* seems to many that *it* would be a good idea to bring *it* back.

In the first sentence, *it* occurs four times and the antecedents are by no means clear. I will enumerate them in turn, with their proper referent. The first *it* refers to *program* in the preceding sentence, not given here; the second *it* refers to *Forum;* and the third and fourth *its,* to *public.* Continuing with the next sentence, the fifth and sixth *its* represent anticipatory subjects; the seventh *it* refers to *Forum* in the preceding sentence.

With a little care we can replace the confusion with a reasonably clear statement.

> The program called *Forum* tried in a rather clumsy way to provide a platform from which the public could criticize the presentations being inflicted on *it.* I believe *it* would be a good idea to bring back this program, but in an improved form.

In the first sentence I use *presentations* to avoid repetition of *programs,* which already occurs once in each sentence. *It* also occurs once in each sentence, in the first with the referent *public* and in the second with an anticipatory function.

We could make a further improvement by eliminating the impersonal *it* altogether, substituting a definite subject, and recasting the sentence. For example, "I believe the situation would be improved if we brought back this program, but in an improved form." Or, "I believe we might advantageously bring back this program. . . ." Always try to eliminate an impersonal *it.* "It seems to me that" means *I believe;* "it is perfectly obvious that" means *obviously;* "it is possible that" means *perhaps.* Often we can substitute an adverb for the indefinite construction, and at other times we can simply strike out the whole clause containing the indefinite *it*, without any substitution.

A sentence that begins "While *it* remains true that the most common cause of obesity is simply overeating, nevertheless . . . " can be markedly improved by a deletion: "While the most common cause of obesity is overeating, nevertheless . . . " The clause "it remains true that" adds less than nothing. The anticipatory *it* is usually easy to eliminate if only we think to do so.

When we worry about the reference of *it*, we must also worry about the reference of other pronouns. Thus,

> Tractors are not seen nor used, for the people cannot afford *them*, and if *they* could, *they* would be utterly useless in the terrain.

In this sentence, *them* raises no problems, for it clearly refers to *tractors*. But the two *theys* are confusing: The author wants the first *they* to refer to *people*, and the second to *tractors* at the beginning of the sentence, but this is not what the sentence actually says. Some change is imperative. I suggest this alternative.

> Tractors are not seen nor used, for the people cannot afford *them* and in any case *they* would be utterly useless in the terrain.

Them refers to *tractors*, and the *they* refers to *them* and thus indirectly to *tractors*. This lacks elegance but at least there is no ambiguity.

Here is a splendid example of confused reference.

> This represented a challenge to our mature values *which* had to be eliminated as soon as possible.

As written, the sentence declares that the *values* must be eliminated, whereas the author intended that the *challenge* should be disposed of. We can bring out the intended reference by a suitable modification.

65

This challenge to our mature values must be eliminated as soon as possible.

A somewhat more complicated example, and one more difficult to correct, comes from a medical case report. The patient was showing progressive improvement.

His temperature became normal but he contracted a urinary tract infection secondary to an indwelling catheter on the tenth hospital day, *which* responded to antibiotics.

What was it that responded to the antibiotics? The hospital *day*—the immediate antecedent—or the *catheter* or the *infection* or the *temperature?* The sense demands that the referent should be the *infection* or possibly the *temperature,* and to bring this out the sentence must be massively revised. I suggest this version.

His temperature became normal but on the tenth hospital day, because of an indwelling catheter, he contracted a urinary tract infection *which* responded to antibiotics.

Whether the *which* should more properly be *that* is a problem I will not discuss here.

One further example,

Discussions following each paper bring out differences of opinion on controversial subjects *which* unify the text into a vigorous and informative treatise.

To what does the *which* refer? The immediately preceding noun is *subjects,* but do the subjects unify anything? Such an interpretation makes no sense; we must seek further. There are several other antecedent nouns, but since *unify* is a plural form, *which* must be plural, and hence its referent must be plural. This requirement eliminates *opinion* or *paper* and leaves either *differences* or *discussions* as the intended term. After a moment of reflection we realize that it is the *discussions* that unify the text. On the principle of placing together the terms that belong together, we might transpose and alter the original sentence into,

> Discussions, which unify the text into a vigorous and informative treatise, follow each paper and bring out differences of opinion on controversial subjects.

But this is rather awkward. To effect a more meaningful improvement we should first try to puzzle out what the author is trying to say. He is talking about the *discussions*, and he points out that these discussions accomplish two things—they bring out differences of opinion and they also unify the text. Why not say so, simply and clearly? All we need do is delete the *which* in the original sentence and substitute *and*.

> Discussions following each paper bring out differences of opinion on controversial subjects and unify the text into a vigorous and informative treatise.

We now have a simple sentence with a single subject and a compound verb. The ambiguity has disappeared, and there is no stumbling over the meaning.

These last examples indicate some of the difficulties that attend the proper use of relative pronouns in general. Our concern about the reference to *it* should extend to the reference of all pronouns. Each should be treated in the same way as *it*, to make certain that the reference is quite unambiguous.

· 4 ·

Editing

In one of its meanings, editing represents deciding whether a given manuscript is suitable for publication. In addition, editing also means the critical examination of a manuscript, with the aim of making it better. This process mends errors of spelling and punctuation, eliminates discrepancies and barbarisms, and generally improves clarity and readability. Editing, in this sense, engages in a smoothing and polishing process. By analogy with the physical act of smoothing and polishing, sometimes merely a fine sandpapering suffices. At other times coarse abrasives may be needed to eliminate disfiguring features.

Editing and revision are not synonymous. In the sense that I use it, editing aims at improving the work of someone else, while revision I would apply to what you yourself have written. Ordinarily it is much easier to note the faults in someone else's work than in your own, for your own faults tend to slither away from your critical vision. As was long ago noted, it is easier to see the mote in your brother's eye than the beam in your own.

Experience in editing, or at least in critically examining the writings of others, makes it easier to approach your own work, see the faults that might otherwise have escaped your attention, and find ways to correct them. The editing of your own writing (revision) I will discuss in Chapter 7.

When I was conducting classes in writing I would give the students a few pages of raw manuscript, that is, manuscript material exactly as it was submitted for publication. The students were asked to edit it as they saw fit. The possession of an editorial pencil seemed to transform a mild, earnest student into a tyrant who first slashed to bits and then reconstructed those bits into a quite different form. When I asked the reason for making the changes, the students would usually say something to the effect that the new form "sounds better." While in given instances this might or might not be true, it ignored an important aspect.

I asked the students, What would an author think when he sees your corrections? Would he recognize the work as his own? After all, it is he who signs it. It is his brainchild and he should be able to recognize his own parenthood. I would then expound my own credo in regard to editing: Preserve the original words and constructions as much as you can, so that the author is never in doubt that *he* has written it. Conduct your editing so that the author, when he sees his article in print, might say to himself, "I didn't realize that I wrote so well."

I had a personal experience that makes this advice quite relevant. Some years ago I took part in a symposium that was scheduled for eventual publication. After I had duly handed in a manuscript, the whole event slipped from my mind. After an interval of some two years, I received in the mail some printed page proofs that, on quick reading, had a certain vague familiarity. I suddenly realized that this represented the manuscript I had read a couple of years before but so massively "edited" that I had trouble recognizing my authorship.

The editing process, I felt, had utterly massacred the original, substituting dreadfully bad constructions to which my name would have been signed. The style directly contravened all the recommendations I had been making for several years. The editor had simply made what changes he wanted and then sent the text to the printer without prior submission to the author. Since the process of publication was too far along to permit any remedy in the page proof, I withdrew the manuscript. This was a flagrant example of utterly irresponsible editing.

The episode emphasizes the problems involved in making a manuscript "better." The author may say that the editorial changes distort the meaning; or that they not only fail to improve the text but introduce severe faults of their own. These problems are very real, especially in journal publication, and to them I will return.

Minor Changes

We should regard a manuscript as a patient who may need surgery. The procedure may be either minor or major, depending on the condition. The editor-surgeon should make only those changes absolutely necessary to render the prose acceptable, and he should deliberately try to keep his alterations to a minimum. Usually a minor operation will suffice. A minor defect needs only minor correction, but some faults demand more substantial intervention.

My concept of minor surgery involves three components: simple deletion; simple substitution; and transposition of a word, phrase, or clause. Let me give some examples.

The first is the simplest possible case, deletion of a few unnecessary words. Here the context has to do with the way a physician—whether treating a patient or engaging in laboratory research—reaches a decision.

The physician constantly deals with evidence. The clinician in practice rests his diagnosis on the basis of evidence that he calls "signs and symptoms"; the medical scientist builds his theories on the basis of evidence drawn from his observations and experiments.

This does not cry aloud for improvement, but it does contain unnecessary words. "Clinician in practice" is tautological. If we delete *in practice*, we eliminate the redundancy and sharpen the contrast between *clinician* and *medical scientist*. Then, the words *the basis of* are redundant; they detract rather than add. With simple deletion of these redundancies the sentence reads:

The physician constantly deals with evidence. The clinician rests his diagnosis on evidence that he calls "signs and symptoms"; the medical scientist builds his theories on evidence drawn from his observations and experiments.

Although the word *evidence* occurs three times, the repetition I regard as deliberate. It adds a desirable emphasis.

The next example also shows unnecessary words—useless verbiage. The cure is a simple excision.

With increasing demands for chemical information on every aspect of all kinds of environmental hazards as it affects man and his environs, the chemical sciences must have a broad, multidisciplinary, and active role in providing man and his world a safer environment than presently now exists.

The need for revision seems obvious, and we can start with the elimination of unnecessary words. These are easy to find. After a few deletions and a simple substitution—an *on* for an *of*—the sentence will read,

With increasing demands for chemical information on environmental hazards, the chemical sciences must have a broad, multidisciplinary, and active role in providing a safer environment.

Only after we have eliminated the excess verbiage do we realize that the sentence, stripped down, shows a hiatus in its reasoning—thus, the chemical sciences can satisfy the demand for information. However, once this information is available, putting it into effect to provide a safer environment is a task for society as a whole. The significance of this thought had been obscured in a cloud of words.

We can distinguish two types of redundancy. In one, the excess words merely say again what has already been said in some other way—a covert repetition. In the second, there are words whose presence adds nothing, whose absence detracts nothing. They merely take up space. The next example illustrates both types. The cure involves not only deletion but also a minor transposition.

This small book edited by Dr. John Doe has as contributors eight highly experienced physicians who have had a great deal of clinical experience in the treatment of blood disease in their respective special areas of expertise.

There is much unnecessary repetition here. The clause "who have had a great deal of clinical experience . . . in their respective special areas of expertise" merely repeats what is concisely expressed in *highly experienced.* If we want to know wherein the experience lies, we find the answer in the phrase *in the treatment of blood diseases.* Deleting the repetitive terms in the sentence, we have,

This small book edited by Dr. John Doe has as contributors eight highly experienced physicians in the treatment of blood disease.

This sentence would be more euphonious if we transposed "physicians" so that it preceded "highly experienced." The rendition would then be,

This small book edited by Dr. John Doe has as contributors eight physicians highly experienced in the treatment of blood diseases.

The next two examples show the need for all three components of minor surgery—deletions, substitution, and transposition.

In the preface we learn that the contributors were asked to provide information for use to [*sic*] the primary care physician as he labors to better understand and treat disease. In addition the book provides the specialist in pediatrics, endocrinology, or metabolism a useful reference source of related fields.

In Chapter 3, I recommended eliminating introductory clauses ending in a *that.* The very first clause in this example, "In the preface we learn that," should go. To be sure, we lose thereby the information that the particular statements occur in the preface (instead of in a numbered chapter) but the value of such information is negligible. A grain of wheat does not outweigh a bushel of chaff.

The first sentence shows not only the redundancy of an introductory clause, but also a barbarism, *for use to,* and a clause that is stilted and precious, "as he labors to better understand." Some simpler expression would be preferable. I suggest editing the first sentence to read,

> The contributors were asked to provide information for the primary care physician to help him better understand and treat disease.

"To help him better understand" does not have the identical sense of the original, but the added compactness more than compensates for the minute change in sense.

The second sentence contains both a direct and an indirect object. What does the book provide? It provides a *reference source.* For whom? For the specialist in the various fields enumerated. In the original version the preposition *for* is implied. To improve the sentence we should first of all place verb and direct object close together: "the book provides a useful reference source." Then where will we put the indirect object, *for the specialist?* It also belongs close to the verb. The solution: Place the indirect object before the verb and the direct object immediately following.

> . . . for the specialist . . . the book provides a useful reference. . . .

The whole passage then reads:

> The contributors were asked to provide information for the primary care physician to help him better understand and treat disease. In addition, for the specialist in pediatrics, endocrinology, or metabolism, the book provides a useful reference source of related fields.

The next example is a little more complex.

> As in the previous editions this text is directed to and intended for those physicians who devote the main part of their professional lives to the care of children, be the physician a pediatrician, general practitioner, school physician, or other.

As noted in Chapter 3 I dislike a construction wherein two prepositions govern a single object. It is not ungrammatical, but since to me it sounds awkward, I try to eliminate that construction when possible. Here the solution is simple in the extreme, for the pair *directed to and intended for* is repetitious. We need merely delete one of the pair: "this text is intended for those physicians."

The rest of the original sentence describes the kind of physician for whom the text is intended, but does so in wordy fashion. The clause "who devote the main part of their professional lives to the care of" can be shortened to "who devote themselves mainly to the care of."

Then, the repetition of *physician* is extremely awkward. As remedy delete the second occurrence and transpose the enumerated classes to be in apposition with the first *physicians*. This transposition requires a few minor changes in grammar. The whole sentence then reads,

> As in the previous editions, this text is intended for those physicians—pediatricians, general practitioners, school physicians, or others—who devote themselves mainly to the care of children.

The last example of what I call minor surgery illustrates the need for simple deletions, simple substitutions, and simple transpositions.

> An almost inconceivable quantity of investigation, over the past several decades, finally has provided insight into some hithertofore mysteries of many crippling degenerative diseases. The information, admirably documented in this work, conveys at least a thread of hope that with this impetus, continued efforts will eventually produce effective therapy for the unfortunate victims of a multitude of degenerative diseases.

Many of the words and phrases, utterly superfluous, we can delete with advantage. The author seems to have adopted the policy, Why say things briefly if you can envelop yourself in a cloud of verbiage? Why use a short word when you can just as well use a long one? The editor has the task of cutting out the excess. For example, *An almost inconceivable amount of investigation* shrieks out for simplification The greatest saving would be achieved by saying merely *Much study.* Or, to use a few more syllables, we might say, *Extensive investigation,* or *A vast amount of study.* Possibilities are many. Then, the words *heretofore mysteries of* can be eliminated with benefit, as can many of the phrases at the end. I suggest that, when the edema has been removed, the sentence might look like this.

Extensive investigation over the past several decades finally has produced insight into many crippling degenerative diseases. The information, admirably documented, provides at least a thread of hope that continued effort will eventually yield effective therapy.

Major Alterations

Minor editorial surgery, involving simple deletions, substitutions, and occasional transposition, is applicable where the author's thought is merely veiled behind clumsy expression. In contrast we have the writing where the thoughts themselves seem confused. We must figure out what the author might have meant—what he might have thought he was saying. If we can penetrate the obscurity, we probably can rephrase the idea in simpler language. Such passages must be handled ruthlessly and require what must be regarded as major surgery. Any such emendations must, of course, be resubmitted to the author for verification, for we cannot always be sure that we have correctly guessed what the author was trying to say.

Here are some examples.

When the medical specialties are compartmentalized in named departments, there are "core areas" which need to be taught and which experience by practice is necessary for absolute mastery, no matter whether the product mounts the academic ladder or contentedly exists as a dispenser of services in city or county, singly or in groups.

After several readings, I believe the author was trying to say this.

Every medical specialty has a core of information that must be taught, but for whose mastery practical experience is necessary.

Reduced to this form, the text reveals two relatively simple ideas, but a lot of work is necessary to extract them from the original convolutions.

The second example has to do with epidemiology and the spread of infection in a community.

> The epidemiology of parasitic infections in human populations is closely related to a number of bionomic and ecological factors which affect the survival and propagation of the causative pathogenic agents. Concomitantly, it is also greatly influenced by social and economic conditions of the population, the state of hygiene and sanitation in the community and the patterns of work and behavior of its members.

There is nothing here that we can call wrong. The sentences are entirely grammatical and the individual words all parse. And yet, despite the technically correct grammar, the writing is heavy and opaque. It reminds me of a soggy biscuit. If we analyze the passage we find an overabundance of words and an overabundance of syllables. The reader gets tired after a single paragraph, and if he had to go on for page after page, he would get very tired. If we wanted to make the style simpler and more appealing, what could we do? We cannot merely cut a word here and there. We would need to go over the passage with minute care, to find a short word for a long one, to cut out unnecessary words—to put the biscuit in the oven and dry it out. The result, however, would no longer be recognizable as the style of the author. We might, for example, come up with something like this.

> The spread of parasitic infection in man depends on many biologic factors that affect the causal agent. Also important are various host factors—social and economic conditions, hygiene and sanitation in the community, and the patterns of work and behavior.

In this rendition I have inserted the words *host factors* to balance *causal agent.*

This degree of editing, although appropriate for short passages, is not feasible for an entire manuscript, nor is it even desirable.

As a matter of practical editorial management, if I were handling this manuscript, I would return it to the author for shortening; to help him, I would revise two or three paragraphs, as models, and suggest that he perform the same type of surgery on the remainder. Here are further examples that require drastic changes, although perhaps less severe than the preceding ones.

Despite this, it is evident that psychological stresses do contribute to the precipitation of allergy attacks and to the aggravation and persistence of clinical symptoms.

By this time, *Despite this, it is evident that* should grate on the reader's ear. For these six words we can substitute the single word *Nevertheless.* For the rest of the sentence we eliminate prepositions by simple deletion and by converting the prepositional phrases into verb forms—for example, *do contribute to the precipitation of* becomes *do precipitate.* The whole revision will then read,

Nevertheless, psychological stresses do precipitate allergy attacks and aggravate clinical symptoms.

A further example, relatively brief, raises instructive problems. The author has compressed into a single sentence two distinct thoughts, and from the standpoint of the grammatical construction, treated them as if they were one. This completely confuses the reference and the meaning of an important adverbial phrase. The sentence reads,

In the past, physicians have rarely evaluated and treated patients suffering from lower esophageal disease with understanding, confidence, and success.

Evaluated and *treated* form a single compound verb. Then we have the all-important adverbial phrase, *with understanding, confidence, and success.* What does it modify? If the two verbs were really synonymous, there would be no problem, but since they are distinct, we must ask whether the tripartite phrase modifies one or the other or both together. When I reflect on what I think the author meant, I conclude that we *evaluate* with *understanding* and *treat* with *confidence* (and if lucky, with *success*).

If this is the correct interpretation (and only the author can say for sure) we must carefully separate the two distinct thoughts. This will require considerable rearrangement. Thus,

> In the past, when patients suffered from lower esophageal disease, physicians rarely evaluated them with understanding or treated them with confidence or success.

I believe that is what the author wanted to say.

My final example raises some points in regard to parallelism. It comes from a book review.

> The author states that the objectives of the text are twofold. First, the book is to demonstrate that nutrition has become a clinical science which, despite its complexity, possesses a logical orderliness based on physiology. Second, the book is not intended to be a reference work but rather a formulation of clinical diagnosis and management founded on physiological principles.

The intent of parallelism is indicated by the words *First* and *Second*. Before dealing with this point we must get rid of certain disfigurements. We delete *The author states that* and we correct the barbarism, *The book is to demonstrate*. Then we try to preserve the parallelism in the clearest and simplest fashion. This requires extensive changes that represent real major editorial surgery. My rendition would be,

> The objectives are twofold: First, to demonstrate that nutrition has become a science based on physiology; and second, to provide a formulation of clinical diagnosis and management founded on physiological principles.

This is the approximate if not the exact equivalent of the original. If the author feels strongly that something important has been omitted, he can reintroduce whatever he thinks necessary, provided he does so without stylistic confusion.

Editorial Niceties

Editing demands a critical attention, a mind constantly alert to discrepancies, to clumsy expressions, to rough spots that interrupt the flow of the prose. The editor must regard the sense of his text and at the same time the mode of expression. He must recognize the passages where the sense becomes obscure or the presentation needs improvement.

The alert editor will, for example, pick up the inadvertent repetition of a word. The author, concentrating on what he is trying to say, may not notice such a repetition. To the editorial eye, not clouded by the original pressure of thought, a word used, say, five times in five successive sentences, will stand out sharply. The editor will then find some way to get rid of the repetition— perhaps by introducing synonyms, or perhaps by recasting the sentence.

Dangles

Another fault that can easily escape the author but that an editor will readily perceive is the dangle—the word or words that sit in isolation, modifying nothing, attached to nothing. Most common is the dangling participle.

> Not possessing a copy of the manuscript, the basis of my translation was the third edition of 1742.

The participle *possessing* does not modify anything. It has no grammatical relationship with the rest of the sentence. The intent is clear: Because *I* did not possess the manuscript, it was *I* who had to use the third edition. The sentence as given, however, does not say this, even though the implication is there. We make the sentence grammatical by saying,

> Because I did not possess a copy of the manuscript, the basis of my translation was the third edition of 1742.

Similarly with the sentence,

> Exploring this possibility, sternal punctures were performed on two other patients.

As it stands, the participle seems to modify the noun *punctures,* which is absurd. The author intended to say,

> Exploring this possibility [*or better,* To explore this possibility] I performed sternal punctures on two other patients.

Note that dangling participles can occur more readily with the passive voice.

In both these instances the author's thoughts ran ahead of his fingers. There was a compression of ideas, the grammar was fractured, and some participial splinters were left over.

Nouns can also dangle.

> An excellent teacher and investigator, his influence spread over all western America.

Teacher and investigator stand isolated, serving no grammatical function. Again the intent is clear. The nouns were to be in apposition with someone (not expressly stated) who spread the influence. The correction may take different forms. We can provide a *he* as the real subject.

> An excellent teacher and investigator, he spread his influence over all western America.

Or we can provide a verb for the isolated and dangling nouns.

> Since he was an excellent teacher and investigator, his influence spread all over western America.

An adverb may also dangle, as with the popular usage of *hopefully:* "Hopefully, it will not rain." Many purists have indicated that this is a grammatical abomination. However, the grammarians may be waging a losing war. If the usage becomes firmly established in popular speech, the grammarians may find it expedient to change their rules and call *hopefully* an "absolute" construction, comparable to the Latin ablative absolute. Into the ramifications of this difficulty I do not wish to go at present.

Metaphors

A further problem has to do with metaphors. A *metaphor* implies a comparison (in contrast to the *simile* that makes a comparison explicit). The metaphor conveys an image wherein one term takes on a function originally associated with some other term. For instance, the music critic, reporting on a concert, might say, "The violins tossed the melody to the clarinets," thus comparing the performance on the concert stage to a game of ball. The melody is the ball and the violinists and clarinetists the players. Other common metaphors are: "Her eyes danced mischieviously," "He made a brilliant speech," and "His mind immediately grasped the point." *Danced, brilliant,* and *grasped* are used metaphorically. Each offers a comparison between terms that in their literal sense have nothing to do with each other but can relate in a figurative sense.

In these examples the metaphor involves only a single word that conveys a single comparison. In contrast, the comparison may extend over more than one term in a continuous fashion. For a sustained metaphor to be effective, the different terms should harmonize, reinforce each other, and build a coherent composite picture.

A fine example of such an extended metaphor I take from Carlyle. He was speaking of his pleasant childhood and the unhappiness that overtook him as he grew up. First he was quite lyrical about the pleasures of early childhood. Then he described what he felt as he grew older.

Green sunny tracts there are still; but intersected by bitter rivulets of tears, here and there stagnating into sour marshes of discontent.

The entire sentence is really a cluster of metaphors held together by a few necessary grammatical terms. All the metaphors harmonize; all contribute to the total picture, with nothing discordant.

Unfortunately, many writers who try to use extended metaphors end with the disastrous product that we call a *mixed metaphor*. Let me give a few examples.

In describing the progress of a musical genius, one author wrote,

His career was really launched in a blaze of critical superlatives after his debut as soloist.

Launching a career is a trite metaphor that in this case compares one stage in a musician's career to one stage in the construction of a ship. But when the author says that a launching took place in a blaze, he has given us a metaphor that is certainly not trite. It is now grotesque.

Another example: The context has to do with a theory that had been under attack. Describing various modifications the theory had undergone, an author declared,

Buttressed with this newly acquired varnish of modernity, it. . . .

This is quite unsurpassed as a mixed metaphor. *Buttressed* indicates a massive support that stabilizes a building and calls to mind the great Gothic cathedrals. *Varnish* refers to a type of paint that provides a smooth glossy surface—a superficial covering. Either *buttress* or *varnish* might create an acceptable metaphor. The difficulty lies in the combination: Paint does not make a good support. We may think, perhaps, of the comment, that a ramshackle house was held together by the wall-to-wall carpeting.

One of my favorite mixed metaphors describes the aggressive leader who "took the bit in his teeth and ran with the ball." Another favorite is that of the successful man who "kept his feet on the ground, his head in the clouds, and his nose to the grindstone."

Alliteration

Another stylistic quirk is alliteration. An author striving to get his thoughts down on paper can place together words that repeat a consonant or vowel several times. For example, "The reader will readily recognize the results . . . ," "The newspaper provided a platform for his opinions," and "He found himself involved in an intensely interesting experiment." The repetitions of the same consonant (or vowel or syllable) three or more times in successive words I find quite grating.

To be sure, many authors do not seem to mind. Some even try, deliberately, to produce alliterative effects in their prose and resent any criticism of this peculiarity. In my own editing, however, I try to get rid of alliteration whenever I become aware of it. We can usually find a synonym that does not contain the offending letter. Thus, in the first example above we can substitute *easily* for *readily*; in the second, *offered* for *provided*; in the third, *a completely absorbing* for *an intensely interesting*. The difficulty lies not in repairing the fault but in becoming aware of it in the first place.

Placement

In grammar school I learned the rudiments of English grammar. One particular example of bad usage made a deep impression that has remained in my memory for over 70 years.

Uncle John went out to feed the cow with an umbrella.

The manifest absurdity proved unforgettable but the reasons for the absurdity were never made clear. In my own thinking I call this an error in placement.

I would offer this general formulation: Terms that are grammatically related should be placed close to each other. The intervention of other words, phrases, or clauses may cause ambiguity and confusion. In the example given, when Uncle John wanted to feed the cows, he took an umbrella. The phrase *with an umbrella* modifies *went,* and not *feed.* Modifiers should be relatively close to whatever they modify. Hence, the sentence should read,

> Uncle John went out with an umbrella to feed the cows.

Still better would be,

> Uncle John took an umbrella when he went out to feed the cows.

Comparable examples, although not so absurd, are often found, if we are sensitized to the fault. Thus, from a book by a popular and very well known writer of fiction, I cull these examples:

> With a shrug he dismissed whatever was troubling him from his mind.

From his mind should follow *dismissed,* and not *troubling.*

> He didn't always hear what one said very well.

Very well should come immediately after *hear,* not *said.*

Problems of placement or togetherness are found even in literary journals of high quality. Thus, one journal published the following thumbnail critique of a book that dealt with a well-known dictator. The following is the entire review, with the names changed.

> It is not necessary to agree with Mr. Smith that the Emperor Jones was the first modern dictator to enjoy his wide-ranging study.

After a certain amount of thought we realize that the critic was trying to say,

> To enjoy Mr. Smith's wide-ranging study it is not necessary to agree with him that the Emperor Jones was the first modern dictator.

In another highbrow journal a drama critic was discussing some modern trends in theater.

Only the willingness of an American audience uncertain of its standards and fearful of being thought less "with it" than the next fellow to sit still and be insulted that sustains today's Theatre of the Absurd.

This requires some reflection before we realize that *willingness* belongs with *to sit still*. Only when we have grasped this can we recast the sentence. One possible formulation would be,

Only when an audience, uncertain of its standards and fearful of being thought less "with it" than the next fellow, is willing to sit still and be insulted, will the Theatre of the Absurd flourish.

This is still far from satisfactory. In my opinion the ideas should be re-formulated in two distinct sentences, but only the author could do this properly.

From the scientific literature I offer another instance. The context deals with earlier days when penicillin was first being used.

Physicians gathered every morning around the bedside of the first patient treated for invariably fatal septicemia with penicillin, as he rapidly recovered.

As written, the author seems to be talking about a new disease, *septicemia with penicillin*. The confusion would disappear if we place *with penicillin* immediately after *treated*.

My final example of faulty placement comes from a newspaper report. It needs no comment.

The bride was given away by her father wearing a gown of white lace with a short train.

· 5 ·

Your Own Writing:
Getting Started

Modes of Writing

There are as many different ways of writing as there are writers. In fiction, for example, the plot obviously has great importance. Some authors plan their whole story with meticulous care. Others—especially those who create detective stories—may prepare only a rough plot for the first few chapters, sit down to write, never look back, and let the story and the characters develop themselves. In many cases the result is sloppy in the extreme, but there are brilliant exceptions. The late Rex Stout, for example, told a newspaper reporter that he never revised his work. His stories, he said, took form while he was writing them, and he sent his typescripts directly to the publisher without revision. The only re-reading he did was the output of the preceding day [1]. The late George Simenon, I believe, had a comparable method of work.

In contrast I would mention P. G. Wodehouse, whose writing flowed so smoothly, and whose understatements and incongruities give such delight. In an interview he said that he rewrote every page nine or ten times [2]. Yet the reader is never aware of the effort involved.

The writers of nonfiction have different but not-unrelated problems. The noted medical historian, Henry Sigerist, gave a detailed account of his own methods. When starting to write a major work, he would first prepare an outline, about a page in length. Then every day he would write in longhand for three hours, from 9:00 A.M. until noon. Using special copy books of folio size, he wrote on the recto only, while the facing left hand page he kept for footnotes and minor changes. In a day he would cover about five recto pages, about seven-hundred words in all. Changes were minor indeed. What he wrote was in virtually final form [3].

In contrast was Rachel Carson, truly a perfectionist. If we assume the initial talent, she said, then writing is "largely a matter of application and hard work, of writing and rewriting endlessly until you are satisfied that you have said what you wanted to say as clearly and simply as possible. For me that usually means many, many revisions" [4].

Sigerist had done an enormous amount of preliminary work before he actually began writing. In such a case we may speak of a gestation period. Indeed he himself declared that when he decided to write a book he felt "pregnant" for a long time. For the most part he ordered his thoughts in his head. When the time came to commit the thoughts to paper, the hard work was already done. Such a mode of composition requires a special type of mind that is rare indeed.

Stout was a novelist, Sigerist, a historian, yet both had an analogous method of working. The hard work of ordering their thoughts took place largely in their heads. On the other hand, with Wodehouse, the novelist, and Carson, the scientist, the effectiveness of their writing demanded first a commitment of thought to paper and then extensive and painful revisions.

These two distinct modes of writing represent, I suggest, polar opposites with a continuum between them. Any given writer will find a place in that continuum, depending on his native endowment and ability, personality, and artistic conscience.

Expository Writing

Although some common problems may attend every type of writing, fiction has special difficulties that I have no competence to discuss. In proffering advice I restrict myself to expository writing and specifically exclude fiction.

When I was in college and took the required English A, the instruction centered around four allegedly distinct types of writing—narration, description, argument, and exposition. These, we were taught, demanded different techniques. For the purposes of this book any such division seems quite inappropriate.

Once we place all fiction to one side, the remaining forms of writing may be studied in various ways. In regard to description the newspaper reporter provides one type, the historian quite another. On the other hand, the "naturalist" describes the so-called natural phenomena, while the physician, reporting a case history, describes the events that affected the patient. The experimental scientist, publishing his results, describes the various manipulations that he performed.

Or, we may turn to interpretations, and discuss the relationships between events. The editorial writer comments on the current happenings. The historian interprets the significance of events in the past. The scientist tries to explain his observations and propound generalizations. Eventually he may offer some comprehensive theory. We have the infinite realms of observation and what are loosely called "facts." We also have the equally infinite realm of conceptual elaboration, ranging from casual opinion to rigorous theory.

These all interpenetrate and may give rise to argument regarding, for example, the accuracy of an alleged fact or the validity of an interpretation. Descriptions and explanations, differences of opinion and the arguments engendered thereby, all form part of expository writing. And when the relationships get more abstract, we enter into philosophy.

We may, however, take a quite different tack. A great deal of expository writing provides information of the "how to do it" variety, that tells us how to accomplish a given end. The cook book is a prime example and so too are the directions telling us, for instance, how to assemble separate components and turn them into the piece of furniture that we saw in the sales room.

Advertising is also a form of expository writing. It contains an exhortatory component, sometimes blatant, sometimes subtle, not ordinarily found in other forms of exposition.

Expository writing, in my opinion, deals with fact, explanation, opinion, relationship, theory, and exhortation. Any individual author may, in any given work, range widely within these areas. In science, for example, a writer may review the literature; indicate his procedures so that anyone may learn "how to do it"; narrate his activities; propound a new theory; dispute the findings and theories of his fellow workers; and also fill out a grant application for additional financial support. All this is exposition. Contrary to what I was taught in English A in college, the separation of writing into four different kinds has no validity.

Initial Stages

While there are many different kinds of expository writing, with certain similarities apparent in all of them, in this and the next two chapters I want to concentrate on the problems attending longer and more sustained efforts, such as scholarly articles intended for publication, term papers to satisfy class assignments, or more laborious works, such as doctoral dissertations and books. All of these involve collection of material, planning, writing, and revision. This enumeration might seem to distinguish four stages, but if we try to keep them clearly separate we commit serious error. For analysis we must break down the writing process into components, but we must recognize their essential interpenetration and basic unity.

Ordinarily expository writing requires the collection of material, whose nature, obviously, will vary according to the nature of the task. For present purposes I will not discuss laboratory experiments or clinical observations but will restrict myself to the problems attending written sources.

With this in mind, once the main topic has been decided upon and approximate limitations set, the author will probably face vast amounts of reading. Traditionally, reading has involved note taking, with summaries or abstracts and verbatim quotations, all duly recorded on cards of uniform size. And as the pile of cards mounts higher and higher, the writer feels that he is making progress.

To the pile of notes drawn directly from printed or manuscript sources, the writer must add the thoughts that come to him at various times. These may flash into his mind as he reads his text or they may arise as he ponders over the notes already taken. With modern technology, the copying of texts in longhand has given way largely to photocopying. Underscoring or highlighting facsimile copies leaves much more time for thinking and reflecting. In this situation jottings of your thoughts and associations are especially important, for while texts do not vanish into nothingness, thoughts do. As you read, a sudden association, a glimmer of relationship, may suddenly occur to you. If not grasped and written down, this may disappear beyond recall. Ideas that have once escaped may never be recaptured. If recorded, and later found to have no value, the notes can always be discarded.

Helpful thoughts may occur during reading, but equally valuable may be those thoughts that well up in a period set aside for deliberate reflection. Notes (or the actual texts) should be repeatedly examined, and the associations that they engender written down and pondered. This process, which I call reflection, is an indispensable part of the writing process.

Reading and reflection involve a circular or, better, a spiral process. Reading leads to reflection, which in turn leads to more reading, which in turn leads to further reflection and new associations. Each turn of the sprial modifies what has gone before. You read over your old notes and you get new ideas that you had not had when your knowledge of the sources was still embryonic. Reflection on the sources can set off an associative reaction, strike a response, lead to some sort of interpretation, fugitive unless recorded.

I would strongly recommend the notation of ideas, not on cards but on uniform-sized scratch paper. I use typewriter paper cut in half. With this you can be utterly profligate without worrying about excessive bulk or cost. Place your notes, thoughts, quotations, queries, and lists of agenda, divided according to topics, in envelopes of appropriate size, suitably identified and filed. Have your scratch pads (or loose sheets on clip boards) constantly available, since useful thoughts can come to you at the oddest times. But in addition to seizing the random thought as it passes by, you must deliberately sit down to think, going over masses of notes, letting them speak to you, and recording what they tell you. Perhaps after a few such thought sessions you will decide to rearrange your approach, discard certain aspects as not relevant, identifying areas that need further data, and generally revise your concepts. If you are writing something quite short you can soon start to write. But if you are engaged on a major project, you should not try to finish your preparation before you begin the task of writing. I would strongly recommend writing preliminary segments, perhaps 200 to 500 words at a time, not in any systematic fashion but as the ideas well up in your mind. These segments are, in a sense, formalized notes. The discipline of putting them down in an orderly fashion provides a structure and coherence that scribbled notes do not have. Such segments may or may not appear in your final draft. Most likely they will find a place, somewhere, but with suitable modifications. Meanwhile you have made your thoughts orderly and ready for revision.

What Are You Trying to Say?

Expository writing involves the problem, What are you really trying to say? a question that on its face seems easy to answer—all you need do is point to the 10 or 20 or 100 pages that you have just written. But for most writers, what they are trying to say and what they actually have said are quite distinct. And all too often what they have said is not at all clear to the reader and not really to the writers themselves. The reasons are many.

The story is told of an experienced author who had already completed a large part of his manuscript. When asked what he was trying to say, he replied, "How do I know what I want to say until my typewriter tells me?" This answer is worth pondering. It implies that, no matter how precise the intention or the original outline, an author is never sure of what he wants to say until he actually gets it down on paper. Even then he is not really sure, but has at least a good inkling, which will become clearer with each rewriting. Regardless of preliminary thought, there is a constant flow of new ideas down through the fingers into the pen or onto the typewriter keys. As we write, new associations appear that did not come to the surface until the writing process started. Often previously unsuspected categories and topics come to mind, as well as many details whose relevance had not previously been suspected. But all this takes place only as the original thoughts get transferred to paper.

We have probably all heard of the novelist who may plan his novel with a definite plot and characterizations, but who finds as he writes that the novel seems to take on a life of its own and that the characters want to do things that he had not originally intended. Rachel Carson dealt with this phenomenon. In reference to her own *The Sea Around Us,* she wrote that the author must not impose himself on his subject. His task, she declared, is to know the subject intimately, to let it fill his mind. Then, at some point, "the subject takes command and the true act of creation begins. . . . The discipline of the writer is to learn to be still and listen to what his subject has to tell him."

Of course, the psychologists speak of the subconscious, of the intellectual activity that goes on without our awareness and comes into consciousness at some future time, often without warning. Unlike Sigerist I find that new ideas are constantly emerging every time I start to write. This is one reason why, when still in the preliminary stage, I like to write in short segments. Something analogous to a fermentative process goes on in the subconscious, whereby "bubbles" continue to rise to the surface over a long period of time. Eventually there comes a time when new thoughts no longer bubble up freely, and that is the moment to start the second phase of expository writing—sitting down and writing.

I maintain that an author cannot answer the question, What are you really trying to say? until he has made a good start on his work and has permitted whatever exists on paper to interact with what is still in his head—thus favoring the fermentative process going on in the subconscious.

The Outline

An important corollary emerges: If we expect an interaction between early written drafts and thoughts that are not yet conscious, then we cannot rigidly plan ahead of time what we are going to say. In more concrete terms this means that we cannot adhere slavishly to an outline. Many books on writing recommend drawing up a meticulous outline before starting to write. These books recommend doing all the preliminary work—all the necessary reading—then preparing the outline and arranging all notes in logical fashion. Then, according to this advice, the work is chiefly done, and all that remains is the actual writing, or, as I would say, putting flesh on the skeleton now so neatly articulated. According to this view the process of writing becomes simplified and can receive the author's undivided attention. He can focus on good grammar and clear expression rather than on content (which is all arranged).

With this viewpoint I must sharply disagree. Some sort of outline is of course essential so that the writer will not lose his way completely. But the process of doing all the preparation first, then placing the thoughts in logical order, and then doing all the writing, may work for some people but I cannot recommend it. The thinking and the writing cannot be sundered, and the notion of preparing a detailed skeleton outline, and then letting that outline determine the final shape of the work, is rarely satisfactory.

We can compare the writing of an essay or a book with the process of gestation, as an embryo develops from its first germ to the full-term baby. An animal does not come into being with a skeleton as the first step. Nature does not first create a skeleton and then add layer upon layer of flesh. Instead, from the moment of conception, an animal is an organic whole that grows, and as it grows, differentiates. If we regard an outline as a skeleton to be fleshed out by elaborating notes arranged in a definite order, then we have a fine procedure for a taxidermist. But the product of a taxidermist is rather lacking in vitality. A writer should create his brainchild along the lines of natural embryogenesis, with progressive differentiation, wherein the different parts react on each other and affect each other as they develop. Of course, he must have a general plan of growth. We do not want a human embryo to turn into an ape somewhere along the line, and if we are breeding rabbits we do not want to end up with guinea pigs. But there is a vast difference between growth according to plan that exhibits plasticity, and growth that accrues on a rigid skeleton.

In one sense the problem is verbal: An outline can be flexible, or it can be rigid. However, in another sense the problem is much more than verbal, for it relates to the very process of creative writing itself. I have two chief objections to writing strictly from an outline. First, it tends to stifle that major aspect of creative writing, revision, or at least to inhibit all but minor changes. And second, the rigid outline, if followed, deflects any benefits from later ideas, fails to nurture them, prevents reaping any profit from maturing thought. By way of example, I would point to the experience I am sure all of us have had: When reading a book of some difficulty, we may underscore or otherwise mark certain passages; if we return to that book after a lapse of time, we may wonder, "Why did I ever mark that, when *this* is so much more significant?" Greater familiarity with the subject has brought new insights, so that what formerly had passed us by, now reveals its full importance; and, conversely, what had once seemed central is now recognized as only tangential. The same process occurs with note-taking. If we go back to the original texts, we may find that our notes missed certain crucial features whose importance we had not recognized at first.

Perhaps all this would come under the category of feedback, a constant interaction between the new and the old, each appropriately modifying the other. Good expository writing demands such feedback, or at least demands scope for its occurrence. Hewing to a rigid outline denies this scope. I would urge flexibility at all points, from the moment that the idea of writing first arises until final completion of the work.

In the writing process there are many problems and many ways of meeting them. Indeed, so numerous are the difficulties that we should rather speak of categories or clusters of problems. I suggest several interrelated categories. One has to do with knowing what you really want to say; a second, with getting it all down on paper; and a third, with trying to say it better. In my view, knowing what you want to say is a process that comes through reading, reflection, and actual writing. Reflection is reinforced through writing; the writing itself, and the thought that emerges therefrom, are in turn accentuated through revision. And then the whole interaction may send you back to do more reading or rereading. Here then are four variables, reading, reflection, writing, and revision. Each affects all the others; each depends to some extent on the others.

In the following chapters I want to offer some suggestions, not for reading (such as discussion would require another whole book) but for the actual writing and subsequent revision.

References

1. *Chicago Daily News*, September 30, 1967.
2. *Time*, February 24, 1976.
3. Sigerist, H. E. Thoughts on the physician's writing and reading. In *Medical Writing* M. D. International Symposia #2. New York: M. D. Publications, 1955, p. 3.
4. Brooks, P. *The House of Life: Rachel Carson on Work.* Boston: Houghton-Mifflin, 1972, pp. 1–3.

· 6 ·

Overcoming Some Difficulties

Whoever tries to explain complex biological phenomena soon appeciates two levels of explanation. The first—the elementary level—rests on simplification. A good teacher who knows his subject well and has a knack of clear expression can make the students feel that they really understand the mechanisms involved. This, however, is only illusion, whereas the second level forsakes abstraction and returns to the real world. Then the students will realize that whatever appears simple and clear is wrong—or at best, utterly incomplete.

The height of ignorance lies in the expression, "It is as simple as that." Apparent simplicity means the failure to appreciate what is really there. Such an attitude, of course, embodies a basic philosophy regarding the nature of the world, a philosophy that all will not share. But since it is my own personal credo I apply it to problems of writing.

The Beginning

Only rarely would anyone try to teach writing through a simplistic formula, but intimations in this direction are not uncommon. In detective stories, for example, a character may have some information he wants to share with the authorities, but is somewhat confused and uncertain how to convey what he wants to say. The kindly detective, trying to put the witness at ease, says gently, "Just begin at the beginning." Such advice, I suggest, is really appropriate only in *Genesis* I : 1 or *John* I : 1.

The detective wanted to facilitate communication. With this in mind it is not difficult to create simplistic formulations for good writing. Thus, one set of directions might be, "Begin at the begin-

96

ning, say what you have to say, and then stop, " a statement that does indeed have a brave helpful sound. Or, from the preceding chapter we might derive another lovely formula for success: Know what you want to say, get it down on paper, and then improve it. If, however, we reflect on what all this actually means, we realize that the exhortations have but little meaning and are not at all helpful.

When does something begin? How do you know what you really want to say? And when have you reached the end? We have seen that knowing what you want to say may be the most difficult part of any given project, while getting it down on paper, by whatever means, may involve grave difficulties. Furthermore, making improvements can be a never-ending process.

Even experienced authors, after agonizing over the best place to start, may struggle endlessly to phrase a given idea in its most effective form. Moreover, they may worry about bringing the work to a graceful end. To make matters worse, while a writer is struggling to say clearly what he thinks he wants to say, he may become aware that his energies are diminishing and that his flow of thought is becoming viscous. He may be showing some stage of writer's block.

Difficulties do not occur in isolation, for any one problem may bring others in its train. In this chapter I will discuss some of these interlocking problems—getting started, overcoming various impediments, and then coming to a suitable conclusion. The problems of revision—improving the modes of expression—I will take up in the next chapter.

A fine example of the interconnection between problems we can find in Camus' well-known work *The Plague*. One of the characters, M. Grand, was writing a book but he could not get beyond the first paragraph. He wanted the work to be flawless, and so he rewrote the first paragraph again and again, spending perhaps a whole day meditating whether a given word expressed the exact sense he had in mind. He kept changing a word or phrase, and he would not go on to the second paragraph until he was completely satisfied with the first. And he was never satisfied. He had written altogether about 50 pages, but they all added up to the first sentence, written over and over with small variations and expansions. *The Plague* is a work of elaborate symbolism, into which I do not want to go. However, this one single episode touches on the problems of getting started, of revision, of writer's block, and of coming to a conclusion.

The advice, that a writer should begin at the beginning, represents flawless logic but bad technique. An effective beginning is always hard to find, and whoever starts off by worrying about it will find himself in the position of M. Grand—devoting enormous effort to getting nowhere. Much more important is turning on the faucet of ideas and getting a free flow that is to be recorded appropriately. Almost certainly the first few paragraphs will be eventually discarded. They serve only as an entering wedge. The time to worry about the beginning is at the end, when the whole work is almost finished. Then, after the author has a reasonably good notion of what he is trying to say, an appropriate beginning can more readily take shape. Only at that point will the introductory material demand effort—and it will indeed be a great deal of effort.

When a writer is planning a major work, my advice would be, don't try to start at the beginning. Be content to just *start*—somewhere. Establish a flow of ideas and keep it going. Even if you already have a fine outline, plan to discard the first few pages and rewrite them (probably several times) when you are virtually finished. Only then will you have a sound perspective.

M. Grand, laboring over his introductory sentences, was seeking perfection of form, a praiseworthy goal, indeed. But an artist does not seek to perfect one small detail when the entire work is still only in his mind. A painter, intending a heroic canvas, would not, as his first step, devote minute attention to a few square inches in one corner.

Writer's Block

A well-prepared writer, once he has gotten under way, will ordinarily keep on going quite fluently—for a while. Indeed, he may congratulate himself on his progress and even begin thinking of finishing the first draft. Sooner or later, however, he will find that his thoughts are coming more slowly. Fluency diminishes, inducing the fear that his creative energies are drying up. All the associations with which his mind once teemed, seem to have vanished. He is coming face to face with writers' block.

On rare occasions that impedence may have a neurotic or psychopathologic background. Much more frequently, however, writer's block, in one or another aspect, is only a common phase of all extended composition.

I suggest two types of block. The more severe I would compare to a stone wall; the less severe, to a morass. When facing the stone wall, the author's mind seems to blank out and simply stop working. In a morass, however, he is floundering, exerting a lot of energy without making forward progress. For a while he may feel that he is saying something, until he realizes that actually he is merely repeating his ideas in different forms. While the words may keep on coming, they no longer clothe new ideas. These two different forms of block require different remedies.

The Stone Wall

You cannot batter down a wall by sheer force, but you can try to get around it by going off in a totally different direction; or you can try to chip away a little of the mortar and make a small crack that will eventually enlarge and permit you to demolish the wall with relative ease.

To go around the wall, you leave whatever topic you are working on and make a fresh start on something quite different. If, for example, you are writing a book and get blocked part way through, you can start on a new chapter, ignoring the blockaded path. After traveling along the new path for a while and establishing a nice flow of ideas in a different direction, you can go back to the blocked portion. You will probably find that most of the wall will have tumbled down by itself and that the remainder causes you little difficulty. Sometimes, when the going is rather tough, you may find yourself working on two or three chapters at a time, passing from one to another according to the flow of ideas. At any sign of impedance you can shift to another chapter without waiting for the flow to come to a total stop.

Sometimes, however, there is no other place to go. You may be working on the last chapter of the book or else writing a paper that cannot be put aside. You must try to get through that wall, somehow. There is a biphasic technique—first, reflect, and second, write. The reflection may not at first seem productive. You take your notes and start to go over them again—and again—and again. Perhaps some of the thoughts you had assigned to one section of your work will appear discordant, and you will want to transfer them to another portion; or rereading some notes may bring to mind a small point that can set off a whole new train of thought. Perhaps you will suddenly realize that you do not have enough evidence on one particular point and you will want to go back to your sources for confirmation or amplification. If nothing like this occurs, do not be discouraged, but keep on meditating. Start again the next day. When thoughts come, as sooner or later they will, jot them down immediately. Do not try to exploit them. For the moment, be content to get them safely on paper.

Meditation you can alternate with writing. Even if you type most of your work, I recommend scribbling by hand when you are trying to overcome a block. Start with a relevant note, or a thought that you had jotted down, or a couple of sentences from the last page or two of the manuscript. And keep the pen moving. You can start by copying what you have already written, writing it again and again, perhaps with an addition of another sentence or two. As you copy, try to make some change in the wording, no matter how small. Try a variation. And the next time you copy it, make a bigger variation—adding a couple of words, finding synonyms, changing the grammatical construction—what you do is not important, so long as you make some sort of change. And soon there will appear a new thought, not necessarily along the same lines you had been working on, but relevant thereto.

You have then achieved a new association and not merely a rewording of the old. You must nurture carefully the new thought, and let it lead you wherever it wants to go. But keep on writing, without worrying about elegance of expression or even grammar. *Keep the pen moving.* You must not worry if the new associations do not have much to do with the original theme from which they arose. They will serve to prime the pump and release a vigorous flow. If that flow leads you away from the original direction, let it carry you along, and after a while you will find that you have a new segment of writing. If it happens to follow the same direction as the original, you are unusually lucky, for most often the break in the blockade will give you something at a distinct tangent, whose "fit" with the remainder may pose a further problem. This new problem, however, will be easier to deal with.

The Morass

At this point you are encountering the second type of impedance, the morass, in which you flounder around. This ordinarily indicates uncertainty and confusion in the author's mind. His thoughts are not clear to himself and will not be clear to any reader. As a simple example we can take the writer who, after expressing a thought, apparently has some degree of inner discomfort. He then starts a new sentence by saying, "In other words . . ." and proceeds to give the same thought in different form. Not infrequently he starts a further sentence by "Or, differently stated . . ." and again gives the same idea in still different words.

The author is aware that he has not expressed himself adequately, and, by repeating his exposition in different words, he is attempting to clarify his ideas in his own mind. The phrase "In other words" is a good sign that he realized he was floundering and tried to achieve clarity. His only mistake was in letting the floundering appear in print. After he had reached some sort of resolution through reworking his ideas, he should then have discarded what he had written and replaced it by a simpler and more compact expression, unequivocally clear (and probably about a third as long). The phrase "in other words" appearing in a text tells us that the author has some artistic conscience but not quite enough.

A somewhat different example we find in prose that is written rapidly. Sometimes an author is in a creative frenzy. If his mind is working at high speed, chains of association may present themselves rapidly, pressuring each other to get on paper. As he writes, the connections between thoughts seem beautifully clear. Yet a few days later the meaning may be unclear even to himself and the original smooth flow may take on a massive obscurity. Not unfamiliar is the writer (often, a poet) who, called on to explain what he had written, ponders deeply and finally admits bafflement. What at one time seemed blindingly clear had become murky. The original writing flowed from associations that had supplied relevance within the stream of ideas. When, however, the associations fell apart and disintegrated, so too did much of the relevance. Only an indigestible lump remained, isolated from the remaining context.

In this situation the author might flounder around, trying to reestablish the original associations and thereby put himself back on solid ground. The wiser course, however, might be to cut his losses and simply eliminate the offending passages.

Sometimes, when a writer realizes that he is trapped in a blind alley, he may try to finesse the difficulty by going off on a different but related train of thought. He continues for several more pages. Then he has the task of combining the different installments of his text so that they will read smoothly. Sometimes he cannot get the segments together. Convinced that the associations exist but lie buried in his subconscious, he starts to dredge. His efforts may have either of two outcomes. He may discover the hidden connection, pinpoint the gap in his exposition, and realize what he must do to fill it in. In this way he will have reestablished a smooth progression from one part to another and restored the unity of his text.

On the other hand, he may continue to flounder until he gets a sudden illumination: The part that seems discordant *is* discordant; the only cure is to eliminate it. He discards a portion as not truly relevant to what he is trying to say. And at once the smooth flow of ideas is reestablished, the unity restored.

Discarding portions of a manuscript is an act of renunciation that may cause the inexperienced writer great anguish. But it is a sacrifice on a worthwhile altar—the altar of organic unity. The discarded portion need not be thrown away. If placed in a "miscellaneous" file it may serve as a nucleus around which later associations may cluster, and perhaps eventually lead to some new creative thought.

Sometimes, when the floundering is quite severe and the author cannot find any way to emerge from the confusion, a more drastic method may help. To any writer who gets mired down, unable to proceed, I recommend this technique: Go over what you have written and summarize each paragraph in a single sentence. If you have trouble in so doing, then probably your paragraphs are poorly constructed and contain discordant ideas. However, do not stop to revise. Jot down a note that here is a spot that needs fixing, but do not try to fix it now.

Carry this procedure through the entire portion of the text that is giving trouble. You will then have a series of topic sentences that indicate, in a stripped-down fashion, what you actually have said. This will probably differ markedly from what you think you said. The rhetoric that elaborates a thought may have obscured the thought itself. This procedure, of making topic sentences, separates the thoughts from the rhetoric (and when you are done you may be surprised at the actual paucity of thought).

When you read over the series of topic sentences, you can easily see if there is a logical continuity of ideas or a faulty development; you can spot digressions and appreciate weaknesses; you can see where further exposition is required. You can readily distinguish the major and the minor subdivisions. You can then regroup the topic sentences, delete some altogether, and transfer others to a different locus.

By reducing your work to topic sentences you can analyze the organization and whatever changes needed to render it more suitable. When the rearrangement finally seems appropriate, then you must rewrite. You may have difficulty, but at least you know where you are trying to go.

When a writer finds that he is going round and round without making any progress, he may try another mode of getting out of the morass. By talking things over with a friendly critic (such as a sympathetic spouse), he can try to express orally what he was laboriously trying to put on paper. If he has devoted enough thought to the subject and is lucky, there may suddenly emerge from his subconscious a simple clear statement of his ideas. And a great light will dawn—"*That* was what I was trying to say all the time; why could I not have said it before?" The answer: The concepts had not yet been sufficiently digested. The act of writing long pages of unclear prose had been part of the process of digestion. Clearer understanding came rather suddenly as the author made the simplest possible oral presentation to a sympathetic listener.

At that point he should quickly write down the few sentences he had just uttered, and the rest will be easy. He discards the obscure pages and rewrites them much more simply and compactly. The floundering has given way to a smooth assurance.

The Ending

Like most complex activities, writing takes place in stages—thus, we collect material, render it orderly, make an outline, write a first draft, and then revise. Each of these subdivisions merges with the next, and we may properly enquire how distinct they really are. Should we plan to complete one before going on to the next?

Here we must separate theoretical from practical considerations. In theory I firmly reject a concept of isolated and discrete stages. Instead I maintain the interpenetration of all parts, with reciprocal influences and continuous interaction, a constant linguistic feedback. Yet as a matter of practical effort, we must sooner or later transfer our deliberate major activity from one stage to another. We must say, in effect, "This present phase is still incomplete but I am going to leave it and go to something different." This involves a change not only in activity but in perspective.

When will the whole process be complete? When will the manuscript be *really* finished? A reasonable answer would be, when the work is considered good enough to send off to an editor or publisher. Yet actually, this is merely a way station on the road to completion. After a suitable interval the manuscript, if not rejected outright, may be returned with an invitation to revise and resubmit. Additional revision, according to the standards of the editor, may finally lead to acceptance. The work has entered a new phase of being finished.

The accepted manuscript is subjected to copy editing, which may entail substantial additional changes. By this time, however, the actual publication, the appearance in print, is in sight. Is this the "real" finish? Publication, I suggest, is by no means the absolute end. All too often the author, on reading the printed version, may think of all the clever things he might have said but didn't. This is the realm of "what might have been," or "what I would have said if only . . ." Sometimes, although relatively infrequently, a second edition makes possible the incorporation of such new material into what had once been considered finished.

Bringing a manuscript to an end is indeed a relative matter. The appearance in cold print is, perhaps, the most reasonable end point. Until that occurs, we must concentrate on the process of revision, which sometimes seems never ending. Some of the specific problems I take up in the next chapter.

· 7 ·

Revising

The word *revision* derives from the Latin *videre*, to see, and the prefix *re-*. More or less literal translations would be, "to look back," or, perhaps, "to regard again." In modern idiom we might think of, "to take another look," or, with slightly altered meaning, "to re-examine." In reference to writing, these translations imply that a revision will find areas that need change, and that the author will have the sensitivity to identify them and the knowledge to correct them. This aspect I would call an artistic conscience—the realization that the work can be improved. Involved here is a sense of values, with a striving to approach closer to some ideal.

The sense of values may have a broad range. On the simplest level would be the correction of manifest faults in spelling and grammar. Such corrections would involve only a minimum artistic conscience—merely the desire to follow accepted rules.

On a more complex level we would progress beyond a simple "right" or "wrong" evaluation. We would enter the realm of "better" or "worse." Here the artistic conscience must be much more strongly developed, so that the author, in the course of rereading, will from time to time have the feeling, "This is not satisfactory, not good enough." The correction no longer depends on mechanically following accepted rules. Instead the writer must engage in comparison, must weigh the relative merits, and decide whether *this* is better than some alternative, or perhaps not as good.

Comparison requires choice between at least two alternatives. Finding them may not be easy. We start with the text as written, which the voice of artistic conscience says is not good enough. The author then faces the problem, *How else can I say it?* Although finding an alternative may entail difficulty, if the author persists, sooner or later some choice will occur to him. Then he has the additional problem of judgment, and deciding whether the alternative is actually *better* than the original.

According to my views, revision of a text has three major components, all interacting with each other. I would distinguish from one another the artistic conscience (which says that the original is not good enough); the search for alternative modes of expression; and then the evaluation of alternatives, with the final decision. Even though the stages are all interconnected, they are more intelligible with individual examination, and I will take them up separately.

Artistic Conscience

In the present context, this term indicates a sensitivity to good and bad writing, along the lines already noted in Chapter 2. Some persons, whom psychologists may call verbally minded, take special delight in the niceties of language, in the well-turned phrase, the clear statement, the precise discrimination, the graceful construction. Others are basically insensitive to such nuances. I would draw a comparison with the appreciation of music. Some individuals, those with a good "musical ear," readily perceive distinctions in pitch, rhythm, and harmony. Others, differently endowed, lack such sensitivity and cannot carry a melody or recognize whether a singer is on pitch.

While natural abilities thus differ, presumably on a genetic basis, even persons weakly endowed can improve their writing with suitable practice, and those with greater initial talent can improve even more. For improvement in writing, an essential ingredient is a critical attitude, deliberately applied toward whatever you read. At first the attention should focus on simple factors—is what you read clear and readily intelligible or obscure and boring? Does the text say something you readily grasp or does it appear like a cloud of words hovering on the page?

Once you identify what you can call good in the writing of others, you try to analyze how the author gets his effects and how his work differs from other writing you regard as bad. An artistic conscience should go hand in hand with critical observation, for even simple analysis of this type will enhance a sensitivity to the qualities of writing. What you like you tend to regard as good, what you dislike, as bad. Such terms are relative, valid for one individual but not necessarily for another. Each reader must search for his own models, and once these are even dimly perceived, he has become partly sensitized to values in writing. He is cultivating deliberate awareness of what he considers good.

With adequate cultivation the author will be in position to examine more effectively his own work. When a rereading induces even a minimum sense of uneasiness we may say that the artistic conscience is slowly developing. Until his artistic conscience is activated, the writer may not even be aware that his work needs improvement. Nevertheless, even after activation has begun, he may still be unable to bring about improvement. The next stage in that process I call the search for alternatives, that is, the search for different modes of expression.

A Search For Alternatives

I have encountered the occasional student for whom the exhortation, "Try to put your ideas into different words," might just as well have been in a foreign language. There was no real comprehension of what I was trying to say. Such a student might have finished an assignment, on which he actually had spent considerable time. Yet once the words were down on paper, they might as well have been set in concrete. He could think of no other way of expressing himself.

In such instances, the root trouble seems to be an inability to "think small." The student was thinking in terms of pages and paragraphs, not of small units, with attention to one word or one sentence at a time.

One method of treatment would provide a small and isolated exercise, divorced from any context. For example, I could take a single interrogative sentence, "*How else can you say this?*" and then demand alternative ways of phrasing that one question. With sufficient reflection we can dredge out many possibilities. Thus:

Can you say it differently?
Can you say it in a different way?
Can you say this in a different manner?
Can you say this in a new way?
Can you express yourself differently?
Can you offer other modes of expression?
Can you put your ideas into different words?
Can you express your ideas in some alternate fashion?

Once the student has grasped the idea, he may go on and on, quite surprised at himself.

This particular exercise has three critical terms, *say*, *it*, and *differently*, and we must find expressions that reproduce their intended sense but in other words. Changing a word may entail some change in grammatical construction. For example, merely using the adjective *different* instead of the adverb *differently*, demands a new construction. The adjective must have a noun to modify, and this in turn would be used in a prepositional phrase. If we attend to the adjectival construction, we readily get synonyms like *new*, or *other*, or *alternate*. We can also find a synonym for the noun that the adjective modifies, such as *manner* or *mode*. Synonyms thus may involve circumlocutions. For the verb *say* we might think of terms such as *offer* or *express yourself*. These, too, will require other changes in the sentence structure; similarly with substituting some noun for the original pronoun *it*.

At this point the question may arise, Of all these alternatives, which is the "best"? The exercise, however, was intentionally designed to prevent that very question. Any judgment of better or worse depends on context, and this had been expressly excluded. The exercise, isolated from any larger relationship, is only a linguistic finger exercise, designed to limber up the student's mind when later he seeks alternative expressions in his own work. He learns to take one word at a time and to find synonyms for it. He begins, also, to appreciate the degree of circumlocution that any substitution may entail.

The next step will emphasize the student's own productions, with their own context. I recommend that he take a short composition, not more than a typescript page in length, and rewrite the page every day for a week. If he has difficulty, he can start with changing a single word and substituting a synonym. He must also look out for alterations in sentence structure that a substitution may require. A well-stocked mind is like a full reservoir, so that turning on the linguistic faucet should produce a good flow of synonyms. If the reservoir is low, the student may profitably consult a thesaurus, such as that of Roget. The primary task is to make the rewritten manuscript different, somehow, from the original.

The next day the student must take the new text, with the changes already made, and repeat the process, introducing further alterations in word choice and sentence structure. This exercise should be repeated daily for a week. Gradually, the student will find that the changes will be not only increasingly extensive but also easier to make.

A word processor can facilitate the work. Changes can be made directly on the screen, with a printout at the end of each session. The next day the student can take the printout, study it carefully, make his further changes, and then transfer these to the screen version. Each day's work must be carefully saved and put aside for the final comparison. The last printout, with its cumulation of changes, must be compared with the initial text. Examination of the progressive alterations will illuminate the whole process of revision, and will reveal the way that critical judgment gradually developed.

Decision: The Sense of "Fit"

I emphasized earlier that different stages of the revision process—the artistic conscience, the search for alternatives, and the evaluations and judgments—are components of a single continuous process, and only the needs of analysis and exposition justify a separation. I could make a comparison, perhaps, with the different integrated motions in swimming. When the integration has occurred, the swimmer no longer thinks of separate movements.

With revisions, once a ready flow of alternatives has developed, the process of selection takes over. Even though several different synonyms may come to mind, only one will be used. Here the author faces the evaluation of better or worse. This activity, I suggest, represents a different aspect of the artistic conscience. This latter has a biphasic nature. First, it tells us that the text as it stands is not good enough, that a change is needed. This gives a sense of unrest. Then, when alternatives do occur, the same artistic conscience must indicate which one has the best sense of *fit*, best resolves that initial unrest and provides the greater satisfaction. You savor each word as it comes to you and consider whether you like it better than the original. If the new term allays the dissatisfaction and induces a sense of rest, you adopt it, at least for the time being.

You have the same reaction toward alternative grammatical constructions. Words can be put together in more than one way. To express a given thought, should you use the active voice or the passive? A subordinate clause or a prepositional phrase? A long sentence or two short sentences? Should you place a given word or phrase in this position or that? When the artistic conscience is sufficiently developed, questions of this sort occur to the reader and contribute to the unrest that must be resolved.

As an analogy I would offer the problem of arranging furniture when you move into a new house. Where should the sofa go? What relation should it have to this chair or that table? You may try it in one position, and yet not be satisfied. You move the sofa a little to the right, or perhaps the left. Then, you go a little distance away and get a perspective. You are satisfied, but the next day you may find that you don't really like it. You make a totally different arrangement, putting the sofa on the other side of the room. You may continue the rearrangement until at one point you finally reach a disposition that seems just right.

You say to yourself, "This is it." There is a gut feeling, the same aesthetic reaction that a painter or photographer has when, composing a picture, he achieves the arrangement that satisfies him. This sense of fit, of aesthetic satisfaction, is not a fixed entity. It can undergo variation, waxing or waning according to circumstances. What was pleasing at one time may no longer satisfy at another. Successive revision of the same text will produce changes that for the moment seemed appropriate but later may be judged not good enough. What was written in emotional turmoil may no longer please when the mood is more somber.

———————————————

When an author has a well-developed artistic conscience, every time he reads over his work he may find something he wants to change. This can be carried to extremes. We have seen how M. Grand, in *The Plague*, carried the process to the stage of neurosis, so that he could not progress beyond his first paragraph. A comparable neurosis, although in a less malignant form, we find in an anecdote (undoubtedly apocryphal) regarding Oscar Wilde. Wilde was indeed a superb stylist. The story goes that, when invited to a weekend house party, he excused himself after breakfast because he wanted to work on a manuscript. He requested to have his lunch sent up to him. When he came down at tea time, his hostess asked him if he had had a productive day. "Oh, yes," replied Wilde, "This morning I inserted a comma. This afternoon I took it out again."

The search for the proper word or phrase or construction, which exactly expresses what the writer has in mind, may indeed be agonizing. Although a given answer may at first seem fitting, some weakness may appear at a later rereading. Then the writer may go through another period of distress, searching for the precise solution. A certain amount of such agonizing is good for the artistic soul, and the reward, although personal, may be intense. An author can derive enormous satisfaction, if, when he rereads something he had written several years before, he realizes that he would not now change a single word.

Such gratification, however, is rare, and should not be the writer's ideal. A hypertrophied artistic conscience in writing may give rise to a neurosis comparable to excessive conscience in matters of hygiene. Handwashing, for example, is a good thing, but when carried to excess it becomes a disease.

How much is too much? For this query there is no answer. To

some extent we learn from precept, but most of all we learn from experience.

Organization

Revision is a means of achieving improvement. So far our discussion of this subject has concentrated on details of style, such as individual words and phrases and grammatical constructions, the form into which the writer casts his thoughts. In contrast to form, however, is content, the ideas that the author wants to express. In expository prose, content varies infinitely and therefore might seem entirely outside the scope of this critique. Such, however, is not the case.

To improve the formal aspects, the author seeks alternative modes of expression, compares them, and makes a deliberate choice. Revision of content, however, requires a different procedure that centers around the text as a work of art. Do the ideas (regardless of what they might be) hang together in a unity, bearing a suitable relation to each other, without discordance? Or are there jarring irrelevancies that interfere with an organic harmony?

I would compare the writer with a photographer making an enlargement from a small-format negative. Using only a portion of his negative, he projects the image on his printing frame, varying the degree of enlargement and moving the negative, until he finds the segment that makes the "best" picture. At some point the composition appears "right," having a balance and yet a suitable emphasis, with nothing discordant. The photographer has called into action his sense of aesthetic "fit."

In a photograph or painting the different components are presented simultaneously. In writing the components are not objects or forms, as in a picture, but ideas that must be expressed in succession. The component ideas, I suggest, should also have the harmonious relation one to another comparable to that which characterizes a good picture.

This aspect I would call an organic unity wherein every part should contribute to the whole, with nothing discordant. In revision of content the author will look for sentences and paragraphs that, however elegant their form, nevertheless appear discordant to the whole. They do not harmonize with the remainder of the text. With ideas, just as with modes of expression (or style), there must be a sense of fit.

An author can never figure out in advance all that he really wants to say. In the process of writing, this is, as the composition progresses, many new ideas should be coming to mind, not present in the original plan (or outline). These new associations, once they have occurred, get expanded and elaborated and, as they do so, tend to go off on tangents. Hence, the original plan, however elegant and unified, gets continually more elaborate and complex. Has the original unity become blurred? During revision, the author must ask himself, Do all these new additions keep to the thread of the exposition? Do they fit into the organic unity of the whole?

During revision the author examines stylistic features, involving the modes of expression. He should also examine the ideas being expressed. Do they all belong together? Do they cohere in relevant fashion? Perhaps some of the ideas should be eliminated from the text, and others transposed to another part. The problem of organization deals with the relationship of ideas. How can the organization be improved?

Unfortunately, I know of no concrete suggestions that could guide the author. Perceptions of relevance or appropriate emphasis are highly personal and will differ for each individual. We must fall back on the artistic conscience, the aesthetics of writing. These can be developed through study and effort—unremitting study, unremitting effort.

Shortening

If I were to identify the single greatest fault in communication, whether written or oral, I would say "wordiness." All too often, a person says at excessive length whatever he wants to tell us. He repeats himself, sometimes in the same words, sometimes in different words, and does not adequately distinguish the important from the trivial. Especially in casual conversation or in writing letters, he tends to follow quite uncritically his train of association. We all recognize the conversational bore, and the long-winded speaker who does not know when to stop. And the fault is equally prevalent in written communication. To say something concisely is vastly more difficult than to say it at length. Brevity requires disciplined effort. This thought was best expressed by an eighteenth-century correspondent who wrote, "If I had more time I would write you a shorter letter." These words should be engraved in the minds of every author.

As an editor I have often received manuscripts that were too long. A simple descriptive term would be *windy*. Often I have suggested to the author that his paper would be acceptable if reduced, say, from 15 pages to 12. In one case that I recall, I received the "revised" version completely retyped and filling 12 pages. The text remained virtually unchanged, however, but the *margins* were vastly smaller! By this maneuver the author had literally carried out my suggestion and returned to me 12 pages of text instead of the original 15.

Another form of shortening is massive deletion, removing whole paragraphs while leaving the intervening text without change. The deletions, enough in the aggregate to bring the pages down to the requested total, nevertheless produce only minimal improvement. If the overall style is flabby and edematous, then, in spite of the deletion, the residual text remains flabby and edematous. "Revision" of this type calls to mind the different possible ways of losing weight. If a physician tells a patient that he must lose 40 pounds, one way of carrying out the doctor's orders is to amputate a leg. This, however, while it eliminates a certain number of pounds, does not really improve the health of the patient. The preferable alternative is to go on a diet.

Dieting is hard work and not very pleasant, and so too is "slimming" a manuscript. It requires careful attention to detail, a line-by-line and word-by-word scrutiny. Early in my professional career I had a most salutary experience that impressed this point upon me. My first major research project, involving two years of work, I had presented in a manuscript of about forty pages. This I sent to the one journal that specialized in papers of the subject matter. The editor, after a decent interval, wrote back that he would gladly publish the manuscript if I would cut it precisely in half.

The letter was indeed discouraging, for I had worked hard on the manuscript and thought it quite readable. To be sure, as I reread it I admitted that if scattered sentences were to disappear, no harm would result. But this simple procedure would not achieve the needed shortening. Something more drastic was necessary. Over a period of some two weeks I subjected the paper to a line-by-line critique, eliminating single words, finding a short word to substitute for a long one, a single word that might take the place of two, a short phrase to replace an entire clause, or a single sentence to express the gist of an entire paragraph.

The work of revision was exhausting and time-consuming, but I finally got the text down to half its original length. And I was rather startled (and somewhat chagrined) when I realized that the final version was much better than the original. For the first time I appreciated the epigram, "Half as long is twice as good." If taken literally this could be rather extreme, but it does point to the generalization that most manuscripts are substantially improved by shortening.

I strongly recommend that when an author revises his work, he should see how much he can eliminate without loss. With a little effort he will find it easy to substitute short words for long ones, to identify redundant phrases and clauses, to cut out rhetorical ornament that glittered when written, but really added nothing to the exposition.

In my writing seminars I emphasized simplicity and clarity. At the end of one seminar a young physician commented to me, "If I made my paper as simple as you want me to, no editor would publish it." I refrained from asking the question, "But what were you really trying to say in your manuscript?" Unfortunately, all too many writers in science and medicine not only lack writing skills, but do not have much to say. They may try to cover up their deficiencies with rhetoric that is supposed to charm the reader but may succeed only in repelling him.

There are, of course, masters of English prose whose work is a delight to read. I think, for example, of the great essayists of the eighteenth, nineteenth, and twentieth centuries, who can take a subject trivial in itself and invest it with interest and charm. Such writers are well worth study. The earnest student will try to find out how they produce their effects, and how their styles differ one from another. An analysis of style is one of the best ways to improve one's own writing.

· 8 ·

Style and Its Analysis

Defining Style

Ordinarily we have little difficulty in recognizing friends and relatives and, even at some little distance, distinguishing them from strangers. If asked, How do you identify a friend? What are the mental processes involved? we would be rather hard pressed to find an answer. We would probably say, in effect, that we have an "intuitive" reaction; and if we try to go beyond this vague reply and identify the perceptual cues involved, we might point to bodily configuration, walk, mode of dress, and the like. Making the discrimination might be easy, but giving the reasons on which we made the judgment is not.

The situation is similar with other modes of discrimination. Suppose we listened to two different pieces of music, neither of which we had ever heard before, one written in the seventeenth century, the other in the late twentieth. If asked, Which is the modern piece? we would have no difficulty in answering. Likewise, if confronted with a Renaissance painting and a modern painting, or an Elizabethan poem and some modern verse, we would have no trouble in discriminating between them, even though they were both completely new to us. We have enough general familiarity with artistic modes that when we must discriminate between something new and something old, we can usually say, *That* has a modern ring to it. And yet we would find difficulty putting into words the reason for our decisions.

If the test involves deciding between two examples of widely different characteristics, the task is quite easy. But think for a moment of the art expert, given a single painting that he has never seen before, who must decide the approximate date when it was painted and the identity of the artist. The expert would know the characteristics that distinguish one era or school from another and, within a given era or school, one artist from another. Ultimately he would probably rely on intuition; after making careful studies he would look at the picture, and look some more, and finally say, It resembles the work of So-and-so. But although the expert might ultimately rely on intuition, he would back this up with specific reasons. He would make explicit the grounds on which he attributed the work to painter A rather than painter B, so that other experts could have a basis for agreement or disagreement.

In all these problems, from the simplest to the most complex, the judgment rests on a knowledge of *style*, a knowledge highly detailed and explicit in the expert, vague and diffuse in most of us. We can apply the same concept to the printed word. Take, for example, the essays called *The Federalist*, published in 1787–1788, so influential in bringing about the ratification of the Constitution. We know that they were all written by Alexander Hamilton, James Madison, and John Jay. We know the specific authorship for most but not all of the essays. In those works whose author is not definitely known literary critics have tried to supply an answer by examining internal evidence, that is, studying the style of the essays in question and comparing the different features with those that characterize each of the three writers. The experts cannot rely merely on dumb intuition; they must give reasons and evidence; and to do this they must be able to analyze the prose in explicit fashion.

What is the *style* that they are trying to analyze? I would offer a definition: Style is the aggregate of qualities that, relative to some particular activity, allows us to discriminate between one person (or group of persons) and some other person (or group). We can distinguish the style of Dürer from that of Bosch, of Picasso from that of the Barbizon school. We can speak of the style of the Imagist poets and contrast it with that of the metaphysical poets; and distinguish the writing of Jonathan Swift from that of Henry James. To make judgments we rely on certain qualities that provide the (approximate) specificity.

Whoever wants to improve his own writing can have no better exercise than to analyze the style of whatever he reads. He should try to identify the qualities that characterize the different kinds of writing with which he comes in contact. For example, why are the directions on the income tax forms so difficult to follow? In the daily newspaper, how does the writing on the sports page differ from that of the editorial page? How does a case report in a medical journal differ stylistically from a short story in a popular magazine? That they do differ is obvious, but it is not so easy to identify the particular qualities that account for the difference.

Writers on writing often give this advice: Read the great classics of literature, the "good" authors, and you will automatically absorb the ability to write well yourself. With all due respect for the eminent writers who have offered this advice, I consider it essentially nonsense, remarkably unhelpful to the struggling author who tries to improve his own communicative skills. What the aspiring author needs is a critical sense and the ability to make discriminations. These he acquires only by deliberate effort, not by passive osmosis.

The aspirant must constantly examine whatever he reads, whether a newspaper, an advertisement, a theater program, a medical journal, or current works of fiction or nonfiction that he reads for pleasure or instruction. And he must constantly ask himself, Do I like it? This query usually has within it a series of overtones— Is it easy to understand? Is it effective? Is it worth saying? Does it grab my attention? Then the aspirant must try to answer the second major question, What accounts for this reaction on my part?

Constant attention to these two queries leads us to the heart of style, for by our answers we can identify qualities of writing. And once we have skill in identifying individual qualities, we can aggregate them into bundless that characterize one or another *kind* of writing. And with further practice we learn to distinguish individual authors according to the combination of qualities that their writings exhibit.

In this chapter I give some examples of strikingly distinct styles, relatively easy to characterize and differing markedly one from the other.

Seventeenth Century Examples

Even in the seventeenth century critics declared that the quality of scientific writing needed improvement. Of course, at this time, there were no professional scientists in the sense that we understand today. In the latter seventeenth century most investigators were amateurs for whom the term *virtuoso* was the popular designation. In 1660 the founding of the Royal Society marked an important step in the organization of scientific activity, and in 1666 the initiation of their journal, *The Philosophical Transactions of the Royal Society*, marked the beginning of modern scientific periodical literature. And the style of writing began to show substantial changes from the literary mode.

Earlier in the century English prose had a rather characteristic wordiness and a convoluted syntax. We think immediately of John Milton and Sir Thomas Browne. Let me give two brief examples from Browne's writing. In the first he discusses the credulity of man as a cause of error. By credulity he means

believing at first ear, what is delivered by others. This is a weakness in the understanding, without examination assenting unto things, which from the Natures and Causes do carry no perswasion; whereby men often swallow falsities for truths, dubiosities for certainties, feasibilities for possibilities, and things impossible as possibilities themselves. Which, through the weakness of the Intellect, and most discoverable in vulgar heads; yet hath it sometimes fallen upon wiser brains, and great advancers of Truth.

In a second passage he discusses the belief that the legs of elephants have no joints.

The hint and ground of this opinion might be the gross and somewhat Cylindrical composure of the legs, the equality and less perceptible disposure of the joints, especially in the former legs of this Animal; they appearing when he standeth, like Pillars of flesh, without any evidence of articulation.

121

We must realize that many of the words are used in a sense different from that of today. Thus, *dubiosity* means *doubt, former* means *front, composure* indicates *composition* or *structure*, and so on. But aside from obsolete usage, the style shows overelaboration and redundancy. Browne generally wrote in complicated sentences with many abstract polysyllabic words. He liked to play with an idea, say it over again in different ways, worry it a little in playful fashion. He was a physician, a man of wit and high intellectual attainments, but he was not a virtuosos, not a scientist.

———————————

If we keep in mind this type of writing, we can appreciate Robert Boyle's views of the style appropriate for scientific communications. In one of his early essays, published in 1661, he declared

> . . . where our design is only to inform readers, not to delight or persuade them, perspicuity ought to be esteemed at least one of the best qualifications of a style; and to affect needless rhetorical ornaments in setting down an experiment, or explicating something abstruse in nature, were little less improper, than it were (for him that designs not to look directly upon the sun itself) to paint the eyeglasses of a telescope, whose clearness is their commendation, and in which even the most delightful colours cannot so much please the eye, as they would hinder the sight.

The comparison between verbal elaborations and the decorating of the lens of a telescope emphasizes his point, that in scientific description clarity is the greatest virtue and that painting unnecessary word-pictures and affecting "needless rhetorical ornaments" are drawbacks. He is condemning useless figures of speech and verbal elaborations, and praising simplicity and clarity.

In studying this passage we are struck by the rhetorical ornaments that he supposedly rejects and the masses of words that he uses to express his thought. He is saying, in effect, that if we want to convery information to readers, we should write simply and clearly—the same advice that is so abundantly offered in the late twentieth century. But advice of this character had as little effect in the seventeenth century as it does in the twentieth.

In 1667 Thomas Sprat wrote a *History of the Royal Society of London*, in which he not only described the history of the society but also indicated some of the benefits produced thereby. The society wanted to correct the "excesses in natural philosophy," one of which was an elaborate, highly convoluted manner of writing. To remedy the situation the Society was:

> most rigorous in putting in execution, the only remedy, that can be found for this extravagance: and that had been, a constant resolution, to reject all the amplifications, digressions, and swellings of style: to return back to the primitive purity, and shortness, when men deliver'd so many things, almost in an equal number of words. They have extracted from all their members, a close, naked, natural way of speaking; positive expressions; clear senses; a native easiness: bringing all things as near the mathematical plainness, as they can: and preferring the language of artizans, countrymen, and merchants, before that, of wits, or scholars. *[Original capitalization omitted; spelling and punctuation retained.]*

But alas for good advice! "Amplifications, digressions, and swellings" are themselves an amplification, digression, and swelling. The whole passage is long-winded and repetitive.

Eventually the journal of the Royal Society, *The Philosophical Transactions*, did have a considerable effect on scientific publications in English, but the exhortations of the society were certainly not immediately effective. Joseph Glanvill, a clergyman member of the Royal Society, published a book in 1668, in which he referred to Sprat's *History*. Said Glanvill,

For their History, that is newly come abroad, gives so full and so accuarate an account of them and their designs, that perhaps it may be superfluous to do more in this, than to recommend that excellent discourse to your perusal, which I do with some more than ordinary zeal and concernment, both because the subject is one of the most weighty and considerable that ever afforded matter to a philosophical pen, and because it is writ in a way of so judicious a gravity, and so prudent and modest an expression, with so much clearness of sense, and such a natural fluency of genuine eloquence: so that I know it will both profit and entertain you. [*I have omitted the italics and the capricious capitalizations of the original.*]

Glanvill, despite his lip service to the precepts of the Royal Society, wrote on the principle, Why say things simply if you can just as easily say them in a wordy and complex manner? There are too many words, most of which contribute little and detract a lot. Instead of "clearness of sense and fluency of genuine eloquence" he might have said "clearly and fluently." Instead of "recommend that excellent discourse to your perusal" he might have said "recommend it."

But here we encounter an important point: Manners of speech are deeply ingrained and cannot be changed merely by good advice. The long-winded modes of expression were deeply rooted in the culture of the seventeenth century. In time a simpler and more graceful style, under the leadership of authors like Dryden, Addison, Swift, and Steele, struggled for dominance, but the change had to come slowly. For scientific writing to improve, a great deal of effort was necessary, and most of the writers did not make any specific effort.

Macaulay

The history of style is an engrossing subject, far too large to take up here. After these few examples of seventeenth-century writing offered here with only brief comment, I will jump to the mid-nineteenth century and take up two contrasting literary figures, Macaulay and Carlyle, whose writings lend themselves readily to specific stylistic analysis. Even though neither science nor medicine is involved, the dissection can help us with our present-day stylistic problems.

Some writers put their words together in such a way that a reader, who has never seen a particular passage before, but has some general knowledge of English literature, can make a fairly good guess as to the author's identity. Macaulay is such an author. Yet when we try to analyze his style we must not assume that his writing is uniform throughout. Any writer may show considerable variation from one work to another, from one period in his life to another, and from one type of prose to another.

Let us look at a few passages from different works of Macaulay. In this first example he is discussing Oliver Goldsmith.

> Minds differ as rivers differ. There are transparent and sparkling rivers from which it is delightful to drink as they flow; to such rivers the minds of such men as Burke and Johnson may be compared. But there are rivers of which the water when first drawn is turbid and noisome, but becomes pellucid as crystal, and delicious to the taste, if it be suffered to stand till it has deposited a sediment; and such a river is a type of the mind of Goldsmith. His first thoughts on every subject were confused even to absurdity; but they required only a little time to work themselves clear. . . .

This is effective writing. It conveys an image, a vigorous picture, although whether that picture is a true one, we must leave to historians. Here we are concerned only with the way Macaulay has put his words together to achieve his rather distinctive style.

We note first of all an extensive use of simile and metaphor. He makes an explicit comparison between minds and rivers and then carries through the comparison in several different respects—the clarity of the water, its taste, the sediment that it might deposit, the process of self-cleaning. In Chapter 4 we saw some of the absurdities that can result when an unskillful writer tries to carry through an extended figure of speech. In Macaulay's passage, however, the metaphors hold. Each facet serves to emphasize the comparison. There is no mixing of the metaphor, and each part of the extended figure is apt.

Then there is a certain hypnotic rhythm. The sentences appear to vary markedly in length, but they are either broken by semicolons or are compound sentences with a coordinate conjunction. Actually, they have the effect of a series of relatively short simple sentences, lightly joined. We readily perceive this if we read the passage aloud, dropping the voice slightly at each semicolon and every time there is an *and* or a *but* preceded by a comma. When we do this we find a succession of simple sentences or quasi-sentences, with an occasional complex sentence thrown in.

This can lead to a certain monotony, both of structure and of rhythm. He achieves a balance through repetition and antithesis— a sort of continuing "on the one hand . . . but on the other." The water is turbid, but it becomes clear. Goldsmith's thoughts were confused, but they too become clear. When this antithetical balance continues for paragraph after paragraph, the net result can be quite tiresome, however effective it may be in small doses. Sometimes when we read Macaulay we get the feeling of a full-rigged sailing ship, rolling from side to side. When we roll to one side, we expect to be carried back . . . and roll again . . . and back . . . and roll again. I would compare Macaulay to a galleon under full sail. The symmetry, sometimes obvious but sometimes subtle and concealed, gives a certain stately quality to the prose, but a quality that can become monotonous.

In this passage I would emphasize the use of adjectives—*transparent, sparkling, delightful, turbid, noisome, pellucid, delicious,* and so on. The color and force of the writing comes from this masterful use of adjectives, while the verbs are relatively drab, with little force. Yet Macaulay has used his adjectives skillfully and avoids the sense of overloading. We do not have that deadly property whereby each noun is encumbered with one or two adjectives. Instead, the adjectives are in large part complements rather than direct modifiers, or else they follow the noun.

Let us examine another passage of a different quality. This is historical narrative, describing the flight of Mary, the wife of James II, together with their infant son.

> The party stole down the back stairs, and embarked in an open skiff. It was a miserable voyage. The night was bleak: the rain fell: the wind roared: the water was rough: at length the boat reached Lambeth; and the fugitives landed near an inn, where a coach and horses were in waiting. Some time elapsed before the horses could be harnessed. Mary, afraid that her face might be known, would not enter the house. She remained with her child, cowering for shelter from the storm under the tower of Lambeth Church, and distracted by terror whenever the ostler approached her with his lantern.

Here we have effective narration, couched in staccato sentences coming in rapid succession like bursts from a machine gun. We do not have the antitheses of the previous passage, the stately rolling back and forth, but we do have a definite rhythm, quite effective in building up suspense.

Then, too, the choice of words is excellent. Macaulay has used forceful adjectives—*miserable, bleak, rough*; and also forceful verbs—*stole, embarked, roared*. Strong color alternates with the more prosaic words that fill in the picture.

With this brief example in mind, let us go back to the expository style. I now give an example that compares the two great British political figures, Fox and Pitt.

> The speeches of Fox owe a great part of their charm to that warmth and softness of heart, that sympathy with human suffering, that admiration for everything great and beautiful, and that hatred of cruelty and injustice, which interest and delight us even in the most defective reports. No person, on the other hand, could hear Pitt without perceiving him to be a man of high, intrepid, and commanding spirit, proudly conscious of his own rectitude and of his

own intellectual superiority, incapable of the low vices of fear and envy, but too prone to feel and to show disdain.

Here we see a return to the rolling antithesis, and we even have an express *on the other hand*. The sentences are rather long, yet their length is due not to a succession of clauses but to a piling up of adjectives and modifying phrases. The whole quotation has only two sentences. The first is complex, with the main verb *owe* and a single subordinate clause with a compound verb, *interest and delight*. The second sentence is simple, with a single subject, *person*, and a single verb, *could hear*. The effect of the passage derives from the succession of nouns and adjectives, used separately or in combination. Sometimes the nouns have preceding adjectives—*high, intrepid, and commanding spirit* and *intellectual superiority*—but the combinations do not become monotonous. However, we must note the tendency of "doubling"—using two different terms with but minor differences between them—*great and beautiful, cruelty and injustice, interest and delight*. This can indeed get monotonous.

In a last example Macaulay is describing the young Samuel Johnson and contrasting his appearance and his mind.

> His cheeks were deeply scarred. He lost for a time the sight of one eye; and he saw but very imperfectly with the other. But the force of his mind overcame every impediment. Indolent as he was, he acquired knowledge with such ease and rapidity, that at every school to which he was sent he was soon the best scholar.

Here, too, although in a somewhat more subtle fashion, we see the balance and the antithesis. There is the same tendency to short simple sentences, with the occasional interposition of complex sentences of greater length. Even the last sentence, with a main clause and two dependent clauses, conveys an antithesis—he was indolent but he readily acquired knowledge. The vigor of this passage does not derive from any one part of speech but inheres in nouns, modifiers, and verbs, in fair balance.

Carlyle

In my writing seminars I always gave the students an excerpt or two from Carlyle and asked them the simple questions, Is it good writing or bad? Do you like it or not? Invariably the majority thought the writing was bad, even though an occasional student might express appreciation. After discussion and careful analysis, however, most of the class would recognize the merits and alter their judgments.

Today very few read Carlyle for pleasure; ordinarily he is read only under the spur of a college assignment. And since, over the years, not one single member of my classes has ever identified Carlyle's unique style, we may guess that very few physicians have been exposed to him.

A liking for Carlyle is definitely an acquired taste. Most modern readers, at first exposure, find his style rather unpleasant, even repulsive. Yet once we get used to his idiosyncrasies, and allow for the unevenness of his writing, we must recognize him as one of the great masters of English prose. Students who seek earnestly to improve their own writing style would do well to study Carlyle attentively.

I will start with a quotation from *The French Revolution*, in which Carlyle discussed the approaching bankruptcy of the kingdom.

How singular this perpetual distress of the royal treasury! And yet it is a thing not more incredible than undeniable. A thing mournfully true; the stumbling-block on which all Ministers successively stumble, and fall. Be it "want of fiscal genius," or some far other want, there is the palpablest discrepancy between Revenue and Expenditure; a Deficit of the Revenue: you must "choke (combler) the Deficit," or else it will swallow you! This is the stern problem; hopeless seemingly as squaring of the circle. . . . Are we breaking down, then, into the black horrors of NATIONAL BANK-RUPTCY?

Great is Bankruptcy: the great bottomless gulf into which all False-hoods, public and private, do sink, disappearing; . . . For Nature is true and not a lie. No lie you can speak or act but it will come, after longer or shorter circulation, like a Bill drawn on Nature's

129

Reality, and be presented there for payment,—with the answer, No effects. Pity only that it often had so long a circulation: that the original forger were so seldom he who bore the final smart of it. Lies, and the burden of evil they bring, are passed on; shifted from back to back, and from rank to rank; and so land ultimately on the dumb lowest rank, who with spade and mattock, with sore heart and empty wallet, daily come into contact with reality, and can pass the cheat no further.

Although in the quotations from the seventeenth century given earlier, I deleted the idiosyncratic capitalizations and italics, I have preserved them in the passage from Carlyle. These diverge from the usual nineteenth-century standards and form part of Carlyle's special style.

As we read the quotation, several things come to mind. The individual words are for the most part relatively short. One- and two-syllable words predominate. The sentences, too, are usually short, but there are many "non-sentences," that is, groups of words that have no verb but are set off as if they were dependent or independent clauses. For example, "This is the stern problem; hopeless seemingly as squaring of the circle." The adjective *hopeless* modifies *problem*, but the semicolon gives it a quasi-independent status that at first hinders our appreciation of the dependent connection. Or again, "A thing mournfully true: the stumbling-block. . . ." The grammatical construction is that of apposition, of *stumbling-block* with *thing*. The punctuation deliberately interrupts the smooth flow. The artful use of apposition is a typical Carlylean device that helps produce his effects.

Most of the words, individually, are simple and familiar; only their combination is unusual. We constantly find unexpected usage—words in relationships we would never have thought of— but when we see what Carlyle has done we realize how appropriate that usage actually is. We also find constructions that surprise us, such as the absence of a verb where we would expect a complete sentence. So, too, with the occasional rarely used word, like *palpablest* instead of the expected *most palpable*. Or the unusual verb forms like "all falsehood . . . do sink, disappearing" where we would expect "do sink and disappear," which give an obvious parallelism. Carlyle deliberately ignores parallelism, but he also avoids the confusion and faulty grammar that so often attend the lack of parallelism, as demonstrated in Chapter 3.

We compared Macaulay to a full-rigged galleon. Carlyle I would compare to a high-powered speed boat, darting here and there, twisting, bucking the waves, making rapid turns, and providing tremendous exhilaration. Nothing would be more hopeless than trying to read Carlyle by any "speed-reading" technique; the result would be chaos indeed. We must read him slowly, for we do not know what to expect. The familiar usages that permit us to absorb the sense through one glance per paragraph are simply not there. Quick glances fail to grasp the significance of his prose; only by slow reading can we appreciate the felicity of his expression.

Carlyle achieved his effects in many ways. Most of his sentences are short, but they show great variety in form and in mode of commencement. One sentence begins with an adverb, another with a conjunction, one with an imperative, another with a pronoun, another with a conjunction, another with a noun, another with an adjective. His nouns, modifiers, and verbs, generally vigorous, convey a sense of freshness. There is nothing hackneyed, nothing flabby. He avoids the monotonous doubling—the use of parallel terms to express slight differences. He does indeed occasionally use pairs, but each member contributes something quite specific. Thus, in the quotation we see *spade and mattock*, but each noun brings up an image of distinctive physical activity—the digging and swinging. Similarly with *sore heart and empty wallet*, indicating, respectively, grief and poverty—far from synonymous.

In his letters Carlyle revealed his mastery of language in a more relaxed but nonetheless effective manner. Here is his description of a visit to Coleridge.

Figure a fat, flabby, incurvated personage, at once short, rotund, and relaxed, with a water mouth, a snuffy nose, a pair of strange brown, timid, yet earnest-looking eyes, a high tapering brow, and a great bush of grey hair; and you have some faint idea of Coleridge.

He is a kind good soul, full of religion and affection and poetry and animal magnetism. . . . But there is no method in his talk: he wanders like a man sailing among many currents, whithersoever his lazy mind directs him; and what is more unpleasant, he preaches, or rather soliloquises. Hence I found him unprofitable, even tedious; but we parted very good friends. . . . I reckon him a man of great and useless genius: a strange, not at all a great man.

What a vivid picture, achieved with such simple means! Most of the words are short and thoroughly familiar, interspersed with a few uncommon ones like *incurvated* and *snuffy*. The sentences are short, relatively, and quite uncomplicated. The force derives from the juxtaposition of common words that we would not ordinarily think of putting together. Four totally disparate nouns, when placed together, offer a remarkable picture: *religion, affection, poetry, magnetism*. The combination is powerful. So too with *unprofitable, even tedious*, and *great and useless genius*. The combinations are superb. In general the forceful words, on which the effects depend, are nouns and adjectives.

I would summarize his style by saying that he achieves a fusion of the incongruous. He gives us the unexpected. He uses words that seemingly—by ordinary usage—do not belong together, but when he uses them we see that they are apt. They convey a precision, and at the same time a freshness that few other writers can match. Basil Willey offers a somewhat different evaluation [1]: "Carlyle can never write urbanely; he is always on the stretch. He sees by flashes and does not think connectedly; summer-lightning, not sunshine, is the light that guides him." With this I can largely agree. Carlyle had an inner vision and, as Willey says, transmuted "any person, scene or object, at a touch, into an emanation of the Carlylean vision."

We certainly would not want our medical writers to imitate Carlyle. What that would be like we will see in Gravenstein's parody later in this chapter. But if we study Carlyle we can gain a sense of the power that inheres in words; we can become dissatisfied with the trite way of saying things, perhaps see things more clearly and offer our descriptions or evaluations in a more effective way.

We will not be afraid to express *ourselves* and avoid some of the mythologies that attend medical writing.

Osler

Let us now turn to a medical author and a specifically medical context. William Osler was a physician of broad culture, whose essays have long been held up to the younger generation as an example of good writing. Today when we read many of these essays, we do indeed find clarity and for the most part a graceful manner of expression. Perhaps there are too many classical allusions for the modern temper, perhaps the choice of words has a certain late Victorian or Edwardian flavor, mildly pompous at times, but the overall result is pleasing.

We should not, however, offer uncritical adulation. We must realize that Osler's style definitely changed—improved—with the passing years. To illustrate this I will give three quotations from three different essays, written several years apart. The first, published in 1889, bore the title *Aequanimitas*, a quality that the good physican should cultivate. In the course of the essay Osler wrote:

> In a true and perfect form, imperturbability is indissolubly associated with wide experience and an intimate knowledge of the varied aspects of disease. With such advantages he is so equipped that no eventuality can disturb the mental equilibrium of the physician; the possibilities are always manifest, and the course of action clear. From its very nature this precious quality is liable to be misinterpreted, and the general accusation of hardness, so often brought against the profession, has here its foundation.

The essay does indeed have a worthwhile message, but the mode of expression, of which this is a fair sample, leaves much to be desired. The striking feature is the devotion to long words of three and four syllables, and the ratio of these to the total number of words is, by modern standards, unusually high. What a mouthful we have in *imperturbability is indissolubly associated!* The whole passage reminds us of Samuel Johnson in his more rigid phases.

A few years later, in 1892, he discussed a favorite theme to which he returned again and again—the need to have clinical instruction in medical school, not to rely merely on lectures, but to bring the student as much as possible into direct contact with patients. Said Osler,

> I would fain dwell upon many other points in the relation of the hospital to the medical school—on the necessity of ample, full and prolonged clinical instruction, and on the importance of bringing the student and the patient into close contact, not through the cloudy knowledge of the amphitheatre, but by means of the accurate, critical knowledge of the wards; on the propriety of encouraging the younger men as instructors and helpers in ward work; and on the duty of hospital physicians and surgeons to contribute to the advance of their art. . . .

Compared with the preceding excerpt this uses a simpler language, with fewer longer words, and yet it still has a pompous character. He does not say things simply and what he does say, important as it is, lacks grace. We realize this if we read the passage aloud. There is no sort of natural rhythm, no smooth flow. Long sentences containing many long words will rarely sound well when read aloud.

Compare this with a passage on a similar theme written almost a dozen years later. Osler was again discussing the medical school curriculum and the need to bring students into early contact with patients. This, we must remember, was written at a time when medical instruction was still largely didactic rather than clinical.

Ask any physician of twenty years' standing how he has become proficient in his art, and he will reply, by constant contact with disease; and he will add that the medicine he learned in the schools was totally different from the medicine he learned at the bedside. The graduate of a quarter of a century ago went out with little practical knowledge, which increased only as his practice increased. In what may be called the natural method of teaching the student begins with the patient, continues with the patient, and ends with the patient, using books and lectures as tools, as means to an end. The student starts, in fact, as a *practitioner.* . . .

How different that is from the earlier quotations! It is clear and forceful and reads much more smoothly. The improvement, I suggest, lies in the relative simplicity of the language. Most words have only one or two syllables. There is no useless repetition, no devotion to doubling of adjectives and nouns that differ only slightly. Adjectives are used much more sparingly. There are many more verbs and verbals. In the next-to-the-last sentence the repetition of *patient* serves a rhetorical function and provides an effective emphasis.

Comparison of these three quotations will provide an insight into the various qualities that relate to style. It is as if Osler revised his own writing and deliberately set out to lighten his style. There is a change, and the change is an improvement.

A Brilliant Parody

I will close this chapter by reprinting most of a brilliant essay, published several years ago in the *Journal of the American Medical Association.* The author, Dr. J. S. Gravenstein, sent me the paper as a contribution to one of *JAMA's* annual Book Numbers, which I had edited for a period of ten years. The title is "New Computer Revolutionizes Writing" [2].

The following is the first report on a new computer, called Hyper-broca, which is capable of translating one English style into another. This unit will affect all writing, in science as well as in fiction. I shall present a brief history of the computer's development, a sample of what the machine can do, and a preview of the changes it might bring and the problems it might produce.

Late in 1958 the directors of the Association of University Authors (AUA) appointed a committee of seven to "study the difficulties inherent in and detracting from multiple author texts (MATs)." Each member of this committee had not only published the required 110 papers, but also contributed to at least four MATs.

Three years later the committee made its report. A single dissenting member wrote a minority report, which merely stated that no inherent difficulties exist with MATs and that careful selection of literate and competent authors guarantees excellent text. The Bible and a modern medical MAT book were cited as examples.

The majority report contains 732 pages and 1,217 references. In addition to the six committee members, 27 contributors contributed.

The most significant part was written by eight philologists who acted as consultants. On the one hand, these gentlemen considered MATs the fulfillment of all literary aspirations and they used analogies such as: "What is a single cymbalist outside an orchestra? What is a lone writer without co-authors?" and "A MAT is nothing but a literary orchestra conducted by an editor, a fabric held together by a common purpose, woven into the pattern of a higher design," and "The editor is the choreographer, the authors dance the parts," and again "The sentences march like soldiers, the paragraphs maneuver like companies, the authors make tactical decisions of battalion commanders, and the editor, the general, determines the strategy."

On the other hand, the critics complained pointedly about the uneven literary quality of MATs. They cited many examples, decried many a poor stylist, but, alas, offered no suggestion how to improve the shortcomings of MATs. One critic wailed: "Ah, could we have Hemingway describe us clearly the mysteries of RNA, could we have Joyce say beautifully but obscurely what Freud and his disciples teach! Ah, would that all professors speak with tongues of Johnson (Samuel), Swift, and Twain!"

Early in 1962 I saw this report and read the critic's cry: "Ah, would that all professors speak with tongues . . . !" At this time I was working with a team of computer specialists. Our computer translated medical texts from German into English. To be specific, into *my* English. Why not into that of Johnson (Samuel)? Or Swift? Or, for that matter, any style we choose? This was February 1962. Today, I can report that we now do have a computer, called Hyperbroca 1, which will translate any English text into the style of classic English authors. . . .

Once we had selected a text to be experimentally "transtylated" (from STYLE and TRANSLATE) and had chosen a number of classic English styles, we prepared vocabularies for every classic author. We then needed a dictionary of "approximate matches," correlating words and phrases in the modern text with words or phrases in the classic styles. Finally, each classic style had to be mathematically defined in the computer's language. To facilitate this task we eventually divided every style into "substyles" and found mathematical expressions for these which in turn were stored magnetically on solid state "stylets," one of several inventions coming out of this project. The stylets are inserted into the computer's first integrating unit, the Broca-1 (for Blend Readout, Override Carried Analogies). We will give all details of the computer, as soon as the patent negotiations are concluded. . . .

For the pilot transtylation we selected authors with distinctive styles representing four centuries of English literature; for the modern English text, a well-written chapter from a recent MAT [on anesthesia]. Rather than take paragraphs from different authors of this MAT, we decided to transtylate into the styles of several classic authors different paragraphs from the same chapter written by Vandam. . . .

Instead of letting chance dictate a style for individual paragraphs, we asked our philologists to suggest a classic author for every section and to write a brief statement explaining their choice. This comment precedes each transtylation. [Each of the original quotations comes from an essay by Vandam, dealing with technical aspects of anesthesia. Two transtylations have been omitted, those of Swift and Milton.]

◆ ◆ ◆

The central theme of this short paragraph by Vandam is blood and equality (or lack of equality). If we wish to emphasize this theme, what tongue would render it better, what style present it more forcefully, than that of Thomas Carlyle (1795–1881), the romantic idealist, the reformer, the herald of heroes?

ORIGINAL
The water/gas and blood/gas coefficients approximate
each other in some instances but are divergent in others.

The reason for this consists of the differing characteristics of blood in relation to the protein and lipoid content, as well as the presence of erythrocytes. The lack of homogeneity of blood, its changing characteristics from individual to individual, as well as species differences, account for the difficulty in establishing uniform partition coefficients to fit all cases.

TRANSTYLATION

And then consider how one vapor residing in gas, will here dissolve in water, there steep itself in blood, only to find the two equally thin. But not in all is blood like water! Nay, thick blood, heavy with cells and fat, may draw some vapors as sand, as dust draws dew. *That*, water never can! And blood has many faces, it lacks uniformity; in each individual, in each species it has its own countenance. With so much diversity, must we not anticipate, nay, indeed demand that one blood differ from the next in its willingness, its capacity to accept a vapor?

◆ ◆ ◆

Men go down. Men are afraid. This is what these paragraphs are about. That would suggest Ernest Hemingway (1898–1961). In addition the quotation from Mushin and others presents the opportunity of using dialogue. Again Hemingway is the logical choice.

ORIGINAL

Among the several anesthetics, there is often a discrepancy in the various signs indicative of depth, as well as a natural variation from person to person. In interpreting these signs the beginner should bear in mind the effects of preanesthetic medication on the signs observed. He should also realize that anoxia or accumulation of carbon dioxide may likewise modify the signs.

Stage I: This has been called the stage of analgesia, or the stage of consciousness with disorientation. It terminates when consciousness is lost. Mushin, relating his own experience, speaks of an increasing disinclination to react to painful stimuli until the pain became almost unbearable. Others describe sensations of remoteness, of falling, drifting, suffocation, and visual and auditory aberration. During this stage, reassurance and suggestion help to allay fears. . . .

TRANSTYLATION

Men are not equal. Some men are put out quickly by the gas, and others fight it and reel back like boxers who have been knocked down but know that they must not stay down for the full count. If you give a man drugs before starting the gas, he goes out faster. Drugs and poor breathing change the way he reacts to the gas. Remember these things if you are a beginner.

Stage I: When the patient is awake, but feels no pain and when he does not know where he is or who he is, we say he is in Stage I.

"I felt heavy under the gas," Mushin said. "My arms were too heavy to move. I knew I had pain but I did not bother to cry out or to move," he said. Then he added, "When the pain grows awfully bad, you move after all."

"I felt far away," someone said. "And still drifting out further."

"Like falling into a manhole and losing your breath," someone else said.

"Yes, your eyes and ears can then fool you," another man said.

We must talk to the patient when he experiences all this in Stage I, and let him know that we are with him so that he is not afraid. *

♦　♦　♦

Excitement, delirium, struggling, as quickly as possible, are key phrases in this paragraph. Exaggerated responses and crass contrasts call for a theatrical style. Macaulay (1800–1859) is the choice.

---

* Note the computer's extensive use of dialog.

ORIGINAL

This is a stage of excitement, delirium, or struggling, in which consciousness is lost and there is uninhibited activity. The onset may be difficult to detect: the entire stage may be passed through quickly if the patient has been well prepared psychologically and with appropriate preanesthetic medication. Likewise, it may be quickly transversed when the rapidly acting anesthetics are given. Breath holding, tachypnea, or hyperventilation may be encountered: the pupils may dilate. Struggling and muscular movement during this stage are among the reasons why patients should be carefully restrained before anesthesia is begun and why an attendant should be at hand during induction. Salivation, swallowing, and vomiting may appear if the patient is allowed to tarry in this stage. The chief reason for rapidly increasing the inhaled partial pressure of anesthetic is to guide the patient through this stage as quickly as possible.

TRANSTYLATION

Then comes the stage in which the patient is mad with excitement, in which he writhes in delirium, mutters without sense, and struggles without inhibition. The onset may be difficult to detect if the patient does not fall into this stage in a precipitous storm, but enters it smoothly; or if not irritating ethers but bland barbiturates are given; or if he is not trembling with fear even before the anesthetic begins, but is calm and sedate from hypnotics. And yet his heart beat may quicken, and his breath may draw fast or else stand still, and his pupils widen. For once, we have reason to ask that the physician not be alone with this patient, but that he have a stout helper; for once force, not persuasion, is required to protect the struggling patient and to prevent injury. If he tarry in this stage, the patient may salivate, he may swallow, he may vomit. The dictates of ambition, of flaunting a smooth induction of anesthesia coincide with the feelings of benevolence toward the patient and with the intentions of guiding him quickly through the dangerous straits of the second stage.

* * *

Admonition and advice are here given by Vandam. Among the classic authors, Johnson (1709–1784) is readily selected as the moralist and critic.

ORIGINAL

Vomiting and swallowing are no longer present, and the tone of the eyelids decreases or disappears. During this stage observation of neurologic signs and reflex responses such as touching the cornea or pinching the skin with forceps should not be used. It is better to observe the operative field and the patient's reaction to surgical stimuli.

TRANSTYLATION

He that is deeply asleep, by whatever means, desires nothing but the continuance of his sleep and is no more solicitous to vomit or swallow than to open his eyes. We do not disturb ourselves with the detection of reflex responses, which do the patient harm, and we willingly and intentionally decline to investigate the effects of touching the cornea or pinching the integument with forceps. From our notion of acceptable practice, it proceeds that we discern more of the patient and his requirements if we study the surgeon's actions and the patient reactions thereto, which shew better than anything I could name the true depth of the patient's coma.

♦ ♦ ♦

The original text has a section heading, "Anesthetic Concentrations in Arterial Blood and in End-expired Air." It concerns the correlation between clinical appearances and laboratory measurements which are often mysterious. It's James Joyce, James Joyce, James Joyce (1882–1941).

ORIGINAL

The clinical signs of anesthesia and electroencephalographic patterns have been correlated with the concentration of anesthetic determined in arterial blood. Arterial puncture and anaerobic withdrawal of a sufficient quantity of blood are followed by chemical or physical methods of analysis. During inhalation anesthesia, continuous analysis of end-expiratory or alveolar air can be performed by withdrawal through the sampling chamber of a gas analyzer, the assumption being that the alveolar gas tension approximates the arterial under normal circumstances.

TRANSTYLATION

Hoopsa, gasablood, hoopsa!

Inward the weary watcher the wavey wiggles that encephalon electrons eminate had the levels of loward lilt learn did. Pulsating pathways' puncture has spat stickly sanguis for trifles tricky troubles tested.

Send us, bright one, light one, send us quickening, quivering breath and her that weighs and it that sways to measure we take and we take and take.

Lo! The sampling chamber!

Three cheers for equality of gas in the hot bed of blood and in the chambers!

Hoopsa, gasablood, hoopsa, hoopsa!

◆   ◆   ◆

The reader will undoubtedly see the fabulous possibilities of transtylation. With our Hyperbroca computer we can provide an acceptable style for every author in a MAT, and we can take a single author text (SAT) and let is sparkle in the tongues of different English masters by switching styles from chapter to chapter, or, for special emphasis, from paragraph to paragraph!

References

1. Willey, B. *Nineteenth Century Studies*. New York: Columbia University Press, 1964, p. 104.
2. Gravenstein, J. S. New computer revolutionizes writing. JAMA 204:51, 1968. (Reprinted by permission of Dr. Gravenstein and the American Medical Association.)

· 9 ·

Dialect and Jargon

Children learn to talk through exposure to the language of their parents and other adults. Early linguistic habits, thus formed by a sort of osmosis, are at first reinforced through peer groups. Later, in school, deliberate instruction will ordinarily induce modifications.

I use the word *dialect* in a broad sense, to identify the mode of speech that characterizes roughly distinguishable groups (of classes or sets). So-called "baby talk" is perhaps the earliest and most transient dialect, soon replaced by more distinct modes of speech that are well ingrained before the child goes to school.

Characteristics

Individual dialects may be characterized in many ways, among others through vocabulary, pronunciation, rhythm, intonation, idioms, and grammatical constructions. All of these reflect, at least initially, what the young child has heard at home and on the street. Residents of Boston, Brooklyn, or Atlanta, for example, are, or at least used to be, readily distinguishable. George Bernard Shaw, in his play, *Pygmalion*, carried this discrimination of speech types to its extreme limits.

Many specific factors affect speech patterns. One category would be geographical isolation. In an earlier period natural barriers, such as mountains or deserts, which limited the mingling of groups, tended to encourage cultural isolation, linguistic inbreeding, and idiosyncratic speech patterns.

Immigration ordinarily helped to modify dialects. Immigrants brought with them their native speech, which they would eventually fuse with the language of their adopted country. The children of the immigrants naturally absorbed the language spoken by their parents but in school learned a different dialect often called "standard English." This second generation was, in a sense, bilingual, speaking the language (or dialect) of the parents and also that of the new country in which they were raised. The third generation would ordinarily lose contact with the dialect of the grandparents.

Modern transportation, together with the mass media—newspapers, movies, radio, and television—helped to break down certain physical and cultural barriers that had contributed to isolation. To some extent, extensive cultural interchange tends to render speech patterns uniform and promote the development of a "standard" language. In another sense, however, diffusion of culture can encourage a more subtle diversity of thought, behavior, and modes of expression.

We can identify particular classes or groups when they share various common properties or engage in certain common activities. These characteristics may have to do with race, age, occupation, education, cultural background, intellectual and social interests, or other features that people may have in common. A group circumscribed by particular factors may also have a recognizably different mode of speech (or dialect). This, when heard, may by association call up other characteristics often present in that group. The use of a dialect suggests that the speaker shares the traits and habits frequently observed in the group. Thus, the mere voice on the telephone, quite apart from what is actually said, may suggest certain properties of the person, such as racial background and degree of education.

Standard English

In any discussion of dialects the question of "standard English" necessarily arises. This too is a dialect, but of a particular group that has a special concern with education. Standard English has a particular relationship with grammar, syntax, pronunciation, and spelling, supposedly connected with instruction in school. Many pupils, however, who have attended school, disregard everything taught there, and their speech and writing abound in slang, barbarisms, grammatical infractions, obscenities, and other usages condemned by teachers and textbooks alike. Perhaps we might say that standard English is the dialect that reflects the views of dictionary-makers and grammarians and then has filtered down into the many persons who have profitably attended school.

Since levels of education vary, we cannot make arbitrary circumscriptions. At some college commencements, for example, the graduating students, as they receive the degree of bachelor of arts, may be told that that they are thereby admitted "into the fellowship of educated men." At one time this may have been valid but now we recognize as illusory the notion that a particular piece of paper can identify an educated person. Equally unsatisfactory, I believe, is any verbal formula. I would, therefore, suggest an admittedly circular and vague definition, that an educated person is one who is generally recognized as an educated person. This is analogous to the definition of an artist, as one who is generally recognized as an artist. Art, then, would be what such a person produces. These views are by no means absurd.

In such a view standard English would be the dialect of a particular class that is recognized as educated. Not only is the membership in that class vague, but so too is the actual dialect that they use. As evidence I would point to the disagreement among lexicographers. This is especially well brought out in *The American Heritage Dictionary of the English Language*, which makes explicit the disagreements among its corps of experts.

Subsidiary Dialects

Traditionally, broad geographical or ethnic distinctions are major factors in creating special dialects. Others result when the activities of particular groups produce special linguistic usages. As examples, bridge players, sports enthusiasts, musicians, lawyers, physicians, and scientists all have their special modes of communication. In the broadest sense a dialect is the language of a particular group, clear to members of that group, but not necessarily to members of a different group. Various terms are used to indicate these specialized modes of speech, such as slang, jargon, cant, and argot, each with its own connotation, but all relate to dialect. They can all involve cultural and social distinctions, as well as linguistic.

Slang and Jargon

Of these various terms I want to pay special attention to slang and jargon and their relation to the standard English. Slang has various characteristics, and no dictionary definition embodies all of them. It has the connotation of something low or vulgar, something substandard. A dictionary, if it prints slang terms, will designate them as such, to show that these words do not have full official approval.

Slang is spontaneous, vigorous, and racy, but lacks elegance. Moreover, it is usually ephemeral. If it becomes accepted into standard language, it then ceases to be slang—it will have improved its status; otherwise it loses its appeal and simply disappears from popular vocabulary. Slang indicates novelty—it is the leading edge of speech. Language constantly changes, and slang, having a broad popular base, embodies new usages and expressions. It creates new words or uses current words in a new sense. Thus, *nerts* is a neologism. On the other hand *lousy*, in its slang usage, invests an old word with a new context and therefore a new meaning.

I suggest one further characteristic of slang: It expresses feelings and emotions rather than conceptual precision. *Nerts* conveys the sense of total rejection but not the grounds that gave rise to the dissatisfaction. It is expressive—unequivocally so—but does not advance rational discourse in any way. Similarly, *lousy* expresses in no uncertain way the reaction of the speaker to the entity in question but does not specify reasons or identify the factors deemed faulty. An audience that has never heard a given slang word will usually have no difficulty in grasping its import, but will gain little intellectual insight into the problem that evoked the slang term. Slang expresses feelings, not ideas.

Jargon is the direct opposite—a language exquisitely precise, using terms in a highly specific sense. It is highly rational, addressed

146

to the intellect and not the emotions; a technical language, intended for a particular group engaged in a particular activity.

In this sense jargon has special relevance to the professions. Ordinarily we think of a profession as a scholarly activity, such as law, medicine, or engineering, but this is only prejudice. Pickpockets and hoboes have their jargon along with their special skills, just as much as do psychiatrists or sociologists. Jargon has a specificity and precision of meaning, intelligible to a limited group but more or less baffling to other groups. Let me give two examples.

Suppose I declare of a particular object, "Or a lion rampant within a double tressure flory counterflory gules." Most people will be completely puzzled. Some, perhaps, will recognize the word *gules* as a heraldic term and then may realize that here we have a technical description which has meaning only for the initiated. I doubt if any of my readers will grasp the significance of what is here written, or recognize it as a precise description of the arms of Scotland. It is indeed possible to describe the same object in words that do not include jargon, but the attempt would be enormously long-winded, would lack precision, and would repel the "in" group and the "out" group alike.

Heraldic jargon is meaningful for those who know it, meaningless for those who do not. I will offer a somewhat less exotic example from botany [1].

> Leaves ovate, obliquely truncate or rarely slightly cordate at base, gradually narrowed and acuminate at apex, finely dentate with apiculate gland-tipped teeth, pubescent above when they unfold with caducous fascicled hairs, and at maturity dark green and glabrous on the upper surface, covered on the lower surface with thick, firmly attached, white or on upper branches often brownish tomentum, and usually furnished with small axillary tufts of rusty brown hairs, 3¼"–5¼" long and 2½"–2¾" wide.

This is the precise description of a particular species of linden leaf. Compare this with a description of the same species, written for the general public and not the technical botanist—the finely toothed leaves are 3.5 to 5 inches long and 2 to 3 inches wide and are densely covered with white to brownish hairs on the lower surfaces.

This brief description does convey the general character and permits the layman to make an identification, but it does not offer the precise discrimination that a professional botanist might need. Jargon serves the professional (or the amateur who shares the expertise of the professional). It has a definite function, and only when that function is ignored should "jargon" carry a pejorative sense. The advantage of jargon as a specialized dialect is not to be questioned.

Dialect and Context

Any single individual will use different dialects according to the context. A physician, for example, uses medical jargon when discussing professional matters with a colleague or writing a paper for publication in a professional journal. When, however, he discusses health problems with a patient, he uses standard English and reduces technical terms to a popular level. The same physician, however, may use sports jargon when attending a football game, and an academic jargon if called on to give a commencement address at the local high school. All of these represent different modes of speech.

We who pass readily from one dialect to another may fail to realize how substantially they can diverge from standard English. We appreciate this, however, if, when speaking to a well educated foreigner with an excellent command of standard English, we try to explain the headlines and stories on the sports pages. There is similar puzzlement if we in America try to follow the technical account of a cricket game. We then realize vividly the difference between "British English" and "American English" as separate dialects, each of which has its own subordinate dialects intermingling.

Since jargon characterizes a particular group, the use of that jargon may have a symbolic function and imply a membership in the class using that dialect. Such an association could be an object of deliberate striving. Thus, a college professor, trying to escape the stigma of pedantry, might deliberately use the argot of the young, to show that he is really "one of the boys"; or sports jargon to indicate that he is not a stuffed shirt. The professor is trying to come down from a rarified to a more popular level.

Jargon may thus be used to suggest familiarity with a specialized group that enjoys popular esteem. Sometimes a layman, wanting to suggest a higher degree of education than actually exists, may use technical terms of medicine or law, scraps of a foreign language, or literary and classical references. Attempting an unfamiliar dialect, however, may actually backfire. The choice of words may be wrong, the pronunciation faulty, idioms improperly used. All these reveal the pretender, who does not really know the dialect.

Changes in Language

Only a dead language stands still. A living language is constantly changing, as new words come into being, new constructions become popular, new modes of expression take hold. At the same time, long-standing rules may fall into disuse and wither. The old dialects undergo slow transformation and replacement.

In language as with any constantly changing activity, there are conservatives who want to preserve the old, and progressives who welcome and promote the new. Invariably the conservatives lose, but in so doing they can maintain a stability that encourages slow and orderly transformations. These take place over a period of centuries so that we become aware of them only when we look back. Thus, the language of Shakespeare and Milton is quite difficult to understand today, and the English of Chaucer is today a foreign language.

In general, the well educated, who have spent much time acquiring linguistic skill and facility, represent the conservatives in language. They have a great investment in the speech patterns that exist, and their dialect identifies them as belonging to a class having education and the status that goes with it. They have a vested interest in maintaining linguistic standards. If the traditional niceties of English should suddenly disappear, a major distinction between educated and uneducated would become blurred.

Modifications, however, will not be denied, and I will draw a parallel with fashions in clothing. Dress, like language, is also constantly changing. This becomes especially striking when we examine, in art museums, the portraits of the sixteenth and seventeenth century upper classes, and then pass to galleries of eighteenth and nineteenth century art and observe the differences. Clothing served to emphasize social and economic distinctions. Even in the present time, although less accurately than two generations ago, the "blue collar" class and the "white collar" class can be usually discriminated. At one time the " best suit" was easily distinguishable at church and evening socials. Sport clothes—garments of more informal character but greater functional advantage—were suitable only in restricted circumstances.

Today, with the dazzling variation in clothes, leisure wear is seen where it was formerly unthinkable. We find sport clothes at church, blue jeans at the opera, and sweaters in very good restaurants. Yet standards still remain. Some restaurants are explicit on their dress code and an invitation bearing the words "black tie" does not apply to blue jeans. Many businesses and institutions set quite strict standards of attire for their employees. Yet even while sanctions enforce many demands for conformity, the overall social pressure in regard to clothing is much diminished.

Entirely comparble is the relaxation in linguistic standards. As a simple but striking example, the familiar four-letter words, although much used in vulgar dialects, were tabu in polite discourse. Now, however, they appear even in polite conversation, as well as in literature and on the stage. They are, however, still barred from television and radio, where ample authority can enforce the ban. The acceptability of change, in language as with dress, has profound roots in the entire social and cultural milieu. Grammarians have little influence in controlling such changes.

Scholarly Dialect

If we take a sufficiently long-distance view of linguistic change, we will find especially fascinating the transformations that slowly affected classical Latin. Over a period of a thousand years, various Romance languages gradually developed, but a debased Latin remained the dialect of the scholarly classes. One feature of the

Renaissance was an attempt to revive classical Latin as the dialect of scholars. The movement lacked vitality and failed, but nevertheless Latin remained the language of scholars until well into the eighteenth century. This was particularly true of medicine, with its sharp class distinctions. Physicians, who formed the elite category of medical practitioners, were learned men. They had to know Latin, for they heard lectures, took examinations, and wrote their textbooks in that language. To be sure, the Latin, as actually used, would have dismayed Cicero, but nevertheless it provided a dialect that identified a particular class. Apothecaries and surgeons, who also engaged in medical practice, were not learned men. They did not know Latin and, with lesser education, their social and professional status was correspondingly less.

However, Latin was fighting a lost cause. By the seventeenth century Latin texts were being translated into the vernacular, and by the latter eighteenth century most original works were published in the native language of the physicians. In the English-speaking countries the medical dialect came much closer to standard English but was by no means identical with it.

Medical Dialects

Two hundred and fifty years ago the language of medicine was usually quite intelligible to the educated layman. To be sure, technical anatomical terms would be an exception, for traditionally the learning of anatomy was a rite of passage from the layman to the physician. But the basic theoretical concepts, then called natural philosophy, could be readily understood by well-educated laymen. By the nineteenth century, however, massive changes were occurring. The specialized sciences of physiology, chemistry, microscopy and microscopic anatomy, pathology, and pharmacology, and later bacteriology, were introducing new specialized concepts and vocabulary.

Actually, this new knowledge was slow in entering the medical curriculum, and for a long time medical education continued in a rather dismal state. Nevertheless, within the century, a new body of knowledge, with its own special dialect, slowly came into being. Eventually it produced a highly technical discipline, quite beyond the grasp of untutored laymen.

The old status of the eighteenth-century physician, as a well-educated man, was changing. In the nineteenth century the physician might have learned a special jargon, but need not have equal competence in standard English. Of course, abundant exceptions come to mind, for many physicians were indeed splendid writers, but overall, the writing skills of the medical profession left much to be desired. This becomes painfully obvious to anyone who reads extensively in the medical literature.

By the mid-twentieth century a new complication was arising. The training of physicians, it was thought, required not only mastery of technical language and its usage, but also something called the scientific attitude. Pundits disregarded the originally sharp distinction between the science and the art of medicine. In the resulting blur many physicians unduly stressed some alleged properties of science. Most important, for our purposes, is so-called objectivity.

The scientist, supposedly, is objective, impartial, and accurate. Objectivity requires that he eliminate any subjective bias and deal only with "facts," objectively presented. Gradually the myth developed that to be objective a scientist must not intrude the first person into his writings. The passive voice, by avoiding the first person, would help eliminate subjectivity and therefore should be cultivated. Colorful language, since it intrudes the personality and bias of the observer, should be eliminated. Quantitative expression, as the ideal language of science, was deemed preferable at all times to qualitative description.

These beliefs, regardless of their validity, were carried over into medicine and helped to determine the form and usage of medical dialect. Medical faculty, who set examples for students and supposedly guided them, were among the worst offenders. One young physician related the following experience. In college he had had the ability to express himself well, only to become frustrated in medical school which emphasized "dry, colorless writing." He mentioned preparing a report in which he described his experiments in enzyme kinetics, involving vast amounts of data. Because he described his experiments in terms like "gargantuan" and "tedious," his professor told him that his paper "was best fit for the readership of *The Ladies Home Journal*" [2]. Undoubtedly the professor thought he was making a devastating comment; actually, he was merely exemplifying the blight that affected medical literature and displaying his own limitations.

As a quite different example, coming under my own observation, I would mention a medical institution world famous for certain research achievements. The department head, while encouraging his residents, established a rule that the word "I" must never appear in reports or even in grant applications. The resulting clumsiness, established by fiat, can well be imagined.

The difficulty, I believe, centers around the blind worship of objectivity and quantification. Some branches of science best express themselves mathematically, and words from ordinary language have a minor role. This does not mean that all branches of science should adopt this ideal. The idolators of quantification in medicine, who want words to be completely neutral, are maintaining a position I believe to be philosophically unsound and subject to all the pitfalls of extreme reductionism.

The passion for quantification may yield apparent precision that may be illusory. We can think, for example, of autopsy protocols, wherein the prosector described what he found. At present we have merely ridicule for the older pathologists who loved similes, especially those referring to foods. We used to read of concretions the size of a grape seed, a tumor the size of a pea, or perhaps a small grapefruit, an inflammation like a purple grape, a mass the size of a tennis ball. Although tennis balls have a uniform size, fruit do not. Today the prosector must measure in centimeters and provide numbers. I wonder whether numbers achieved through a celluloid ruler (or even naked eye estimation) produce any lesser degree of error for the reader than does a comparison with green peas.

This leads to the more important point, just how much of the prevalent quantitation has any real point? And to what degree is the collection of numbers carried out for the sake of collecting numbers? Without denying the importance of quantitation, I suggest that medicine might be better off if we replaced much of our quantitation and its supposed precision, with expressive qualitative words that reflected awareness of the world around us. Relevance and comparison can mean more than figures. Quantitation is obviously important, but I deny that it is more important than the judicious use of language.

Too often medical writing is stilted and repulsive. Under the cloak of "science" the various defects are first defended and then reevaluated as positive merits. Medicine does indeed require a technical language, but there is no necessity for a technical dialect to go hand in hand with bad writing. Furthermore, there is no need to confuse obscurity of expression with profundity of thought.

References

1. Sargent, C. S. *Manual of the Trees of North America* (2nd ed.). New York: Dover, 1965. Vol. 2, p. 745.
2. Letter to the editor. *New Engl. J. Med.* 287: 941, 1972.

· 10 ·

Context, Synonyms, and Translation

English draws its words from many sources, in particular from the
Greek, Latin, and Romance languages on the one hand and from
the Teutonic languages on the other. All have contributed to the
richness of modern English as a medium of expression.
The user of English has at his disposal a wealth of synonyms,
among which he can find alternative ways of expressing a given
idea. Yet no two words will have meanings the same in all respects;
somewhere along the line they diverge; synonyms provide a simi-
larity in some respects but not in others. As the *Oxford English
Dictionary* indicates, synonyms have "the same general sense," but
each of them has meanings not shared by the others and exhibits
different shades of meaning in different contexts. Under certain
circumstances the meanings overlap; in others they diverge. The
O.E.D. gives an example from Prescott's *Philip II*: "The name of
soldier is synonymous with that of marauder." Clearly, there are
many soldiers who are not marauders and many marauders who are
not soldiers. However, during the historical era of Philip II, soldiers
behaved outrageously and plundered wantonly. Under those circumstances the meanings of *soldier* and *marauder* overlapped, but
in other contexts, other circumstances, they did not.
  Context means literally a weaving together. It implies a union of
parts into a whole, whereby the meaning of the whole determines
the meaning of an individual part. As an illustration of this we
might think of words with the same spelling but different pronun-
ciations. The sentence as a whole tells us which meaning is appropriate. Thus, *lead* in one context is a noun indicating a particular heavy metal; in another it is a verb, meaning "to conduct" or
"to guide." *Let* in one context means "to permit"; in another it

155

describes a feature in tennis wherein the serve has been hindered and the point must be played again.

Words are synonyms only when there is a partial overlap of contexts. In many situations, for example, *belly* and *abdomen* are synonyms. "The patient had a pain in the belly" and "The patient had a pain in the abdomen" have the same medical significance. But in a different usage *belly* and *abdomen* are no longer synonyms. We might speak of the belly of a sail or a violin, but not the abdomen of a sail or a violin. And abdomen dance is not interchangeable with belly dance.

Through usage words extend their meanings into different contexts, get settled there, and take on a new sense, often metaphorical. Think, for example, of the modern, more or less slang, significance of *square* or *camp*.

Words from different roots that at one time had similar meanings may subsequently diverge. Take, for instance, *gut* and *intestine*. *Gut*, of Teutonic origin, meant the contents of the abdominal cavity, the entrails. Then the word became directed to a particular entrail, the lower alimentary tract. But by extension it came to have other meanings, including violin strings, the silken fiber from the intestine of a silkworm, and a narrow channel or passage, as, a channel of water. On the other hand, *intestine* comes from the Latin *intus*, meaning *within*. It referred to the lower part of the alimentary canal but did not acquire a host of accessory meanings. *Gut* and *intestine* are most certainly synonyms for the lower alimentary tract, but the congruence of meaning stops there.

We might think of synonyms as intersecting circles. The portions that intersect represent the identity of meanings, and in that area the words are interchangeable. The portions of the circles that do not intersect represent the meanings unique for each, not applicable to other contexts. We might think of each circle as having a flavor, an indefinite aura, a composite imagery derived from all the varied usages. The flavor of the whole affects that part of the circle acting as synonym. The word *square*, for example, applied to the highly conservative person out of touch with modern trends, conveys a definite image. The word calls up the properties of a geometric figure—something stable, with sharp angles. The person we call square seems to take on these properties as we use the word. Different synonyms will each bring their own metaphorical flavor that affects the total prose picture.

***

Synonym and context are essential terms in translation. When we learn a foreign language we start with the rudiments of grammar and an elementary vocabulary. We have lists of words in the one language and a list of equivalents in the other. The two lists represent synonyms. Then, after gaining a little overall familiarity, we start on an elementary reader. These, ordinarily, have a vocabulary in the back, giving in alphabetical order the foreign words, each with its English equivalent.

The beginning student may get the idea of a one-to-one equivalence—only one right English word for each foreign word. He ignores the concept that synonyms—equivalence—depend entirely on context. And if you find a different context, you cannot assume that the two words, the foreign and the English, are still equivalent.

A reverse example of this I encountered in a small provincial French hotel whose owner had a limited knowledge of English. Prominently displayed in the room was a sign in English that began, "The direction does not answer for things of value. . . ." The source of his difficulty is easy to find. The French *direction* does indeed correspond to *direction* in English, but only in a particular context. For the sense that the owner intended, the proper translation of *direction* would be *management*. Similarly, the word *répondre* does indeed sometimes mean *to answer*, but in a different context it can mean *to be responsible for*. What the owner had said to himself in French would be rendered in English as "The management is not responsible for valuables. . . ." We cannot translate one language into another without thoroughly understanding that context determines the sense.

The situation lends itself to an amusing game. Take a sentence in a foreign language, look up every word in a good dictionary, and then, while preserving the grammatical structure, use in your translation English words found in the dictionary but intended for a different usage. Such a disregard of context results in amusing nonsense. Here is an example taken from La Mettrie's *L'homme machine*.

> From what I have just said the best society for a husband of inspiration is his own, if he does not detect a similar one.

This, I am sure, baffles the understanding. The "proper" translation is,

> From what I have just said, it follows that a brilliant man is his own best company, unless he can find other company of the same sort.

The original French, from which the translation is taken, reads

> Ce que je viens de dire prouve que la meilleure compagnie pour un homme d'esprit, est la sienne, s'il n'en trouve une semblable.

If my translation were intended seriously, it would be considered atrocious. Unfortunately, some translations of scholarly works, seriously offered to the public, are almost as bad, show a profound disregard of context, and yield a result that at best is confusing, at worst utterly wrong.

Here, as an example, is a published translation from the German. The subject matter is the so-called healing power of nature and the changes that this concept had undergone.

> Here the history of the conception of nature and its numerous changes cannot be considered in detail, only it should be said that the representation of nature as an almost personal, consciously purposeful managing nature, standing above the material, no longer seemed maintainable since Galileo, Bacon, and Cartesius, rebuilding anew on the basis of discovery, had overthrown the scholastic-Aristotelian world conception.

After much effort the reader may get a rough impression of what the author intended but certainly not a precise account of the original ideas. At best the wording is clumsy, with less than optimal rendition of particular German words, and in two places the translation is wrong. Before offering a better translation I give the original German text.

Es kann hier nicht auf die Geschichte des Naturbegriffes und seine mannigfachen Wandlungen eingegangen werden, nur das sei gesagt, dass die Vorstellung der Natur als eines beinahe persönlich gedachten, über der Materie stehenden, bewusst zweckmässig handelnden Wesens nicht mehr haltbar schien, seitdem Galilei, Bacon, Cartesius von Grund auf die Erkenntnis neu aufgebaut, den Sturz der Scholastisch-aristotelischen Weltanschauung herbeigeführt hatten.

The word *material* in the published translation is wrong. It should be *Matter*, referring specifically to the Aristotelian conception. Then, "rebuilding anew on the basis of discovery," also wrong, misconstrues the German words. Furthermore, even where the rendition is technically not incorrect, it is awkward and confusing. For comparison with the published version I offer a different translation, with a more precise choice of English words, better adapted to the context of the original.

We cannot here take up the history of the Concept of Nature and its many transformations. Let us say only that the idea of Nature, regarded as an almost personalized Essence standing above Matter, conscious, and acting in a purposeful manner, appears no longer tenable, ever since Galileo, Bacon, and Descartes, on the basis of new-found knowledge, had brought about the collapse of the scholastic and Aristotelian world view.

The principle of translation is to stay as close to the original sense as possible, and yet produce idiomatic English. The translator must choose a word that reflects the original meaning, fits into the context, and is completely idiomatic.

I could give many instances of thoroughly bad translation, so bad, often, as to be incomprehensible. While examples abound today, the defects were much more widespread in earlier times. In the past, especially in the seventeenth and eighteenth centuries, translation was a drudge job, a means whereby an author could eke out a bare subsistence and provide himself with an income that, however meager, would still permit him to write his play or his poems. A publisher might sniff out a market for an English version of some continental work and then find someone to provide the translation. Grub Street was the term to describe not so much a physical locus as a general activity. Publishers would commission poverty-stricken authors to translate various foreign works at page rates. There was no standard of excellence to be met, no critical evaluation of the manuscript before it was printed.

The drudge who did the work might or might not be knowledgeable in the particular field. He would have, say, a knowledge of Latin or French, sufficient to turn out a rapid translation that bore some relationship to the original. Speed was of the essence, since payment was by the page. With this method of payment, and with no critical examination of the result, the translator had no incentive to make an accurate rendition.

As a medical historian I have had occasion to study intensively the writings of seventeenth- and eighteenth-century physicians. Most of them wrote in Latin. Many of the major texts had been translated into English, but a modern scholar needs only a brief exposure to these translations to appreciate their frequent obscurity. With some exceptions the available English renditions gave a vague (even though fine-sounding) exposition that might serve for generalities but have little value for rigorous analysis. For the most part the English editions served only as "finders," to give a general sense that this or that passage was probably important. To appreciate the fine points the reader would have to go to the original Latin. Of the great medical classics of that era, originally written in Latin, only a small proportion had a satisfactory version in English.

If we try to analyze why the translations as a class are so bad, we can note several causal factors. First, many of the translators were not competent in the particular area of scholarship. An eighteenth-century hack writer well versed in Juvenal or Lucan, would not, a priori, be expected to understand the subtleties of the mechanical philosophy or its application to physiology. To produce a good translation a writer must have a sound knowledge of the subject matter involved. Many translators of medical works, for example, were neither physicians nor scientists; they could not grasp subtleties of expression or fine points of doctrine. But even assuming that a translator has a thorough command of the subject matter in question, he also needs a mastery of the English language. He must recognize the shades of meaning that the original terms involve, and then express these in English prose that will convey the original distinction. Indeed, it is more important for a translator to be a master of the language into which the work is to be rendered than a master of the original language.

As a third requisite I suggest that the translator must avoid haste. Sometimes an author will dash off an original composition at white heat and record his inspiration while it is still glowing in his mind. Translation, however, can never be accomplished in passion. It requires deliberation, scrutiny, and questioning: Is this word or that word best under the circumstances? A decision may require considerable thought and time.

Quite commonly we encounter the question, How *literal* should a translation be? To what degree should there be a word-for-word rendition? The word *literal* embodies gradations depending on context and purpose. The *idiom*, for example, is a rock on which all translations can founder. Take the simple query, "How do you do?" To attempt a word-for-word translation into another language would be nonsense. Yet most languages have an equivalent question, with an identical context and purpose. In translating an idiom we try to give an equivalent, and an equivalent is by no means a literal rendition.

Differences in grammar offer a further insurmountable barrier to literal translation. Think, for a moment, of the reflexive constructions so common in languages other than English, or—an example I have used before—of the long chains of modifiers that can precede a noun in German. These modifiers may themselves have modifiers and qualifications that would make any word-for-word rendition intolerable. Again we must fall back on the notion of equivalence—getting holding of the sense and rendering that sense in a form that will be idiomatic, properly grammatical, and yet close to the original.

Most students of Latin have had experience with the interlinear translation, more commonly known, perhaps, as a pony or trot. This is the closest approximation to a literal translation. Above each Latin word is an English word in translation, but the order of the words remains Latin. To offer a respectable translation the student must rearrange the words into an order appropriate for English.

We can contrast the interlinear translation of Caesar or Cicero with the scholarly texts of the Loeb Library, which offer the original Latin (or Greek) on one page and the English translation on the facing page. These scholarly renditions do not try to be literal but they are remarkably close. They provide an equivalent in English for what the author had said in the original language.

To be sure, in a few simple examples the equivalent and the literal will coincide. "The pen of my aunt is black" can be translated literally into almost any foreign language, and sentences of this type are useful as introductory exercises. But the literal and the equivalent soon diverge when we progress into more complex speech or into what we may properly call literature. If we are translating poetry, or drama, or a novel, or a scholarly treatise, or a political speech, or a news report, what does *equivalent* mean? Each of these modes of language has a different purpose, a different context, and these will affect the character of the translation.

How, for example, should we translate poetry? Should the translation try to preserve the rhyme scheme of the original, or forego rhyme while still remaining metrical? In either case, should the translation preserve the original meter? Or should the rendition be in prose? To illustrate variations in the concept of *equivalence*, we can think of the numerous translations of the *Iliad* or the *Inferno*, Goethe's *Faust* or Molière's verse comedies.

Complete equivalence in all respects is impossible. Something must give. One translator, wanting to keep the original rhyme scheme, will diverge from what the author actually said. Another translator, who wants to keep closer to the original text, will give up the rhyme and translate into free verse or prose. In any case the translator will claim that he keeps to the spirit of the original. But *spirit* will mean different things to different people, and therefore different translations of the same poem will vary tremendously. Translating a work of fiction offers problems that are somewhat less severe than those of translating poetry but still comparable. In fiction, particular locale, peculiarities of social behavior and adaptation, and colloquial speech can play an important role in narration. The translator must convert the idioms of one language into those of another: He must render the situations and behavior patterns meaningful for an audience that may have a different culture. What to do, for example, with patterns of speech and behavior, immediately understood by the original audience but perhaps rather obscure for readers far removed in time and space? These problems, especially acute in translating fiction, may also be troublesome in translating expository prose.

An unskilled translator may use vogue terms that enjoy a brief popularity but which, to a later generation, will seem stilted and even ludicrous. Such a translator has tried too hard to use idioms of the new language to express the ideas and actions of the old. Yet if he sticks too closely to the original words, his effort may seem wooden, lifeless. A good translation will always diverge from any literal rendition; but even though to some extent free, it will nevertheless be *close*. We cannot reduce the degree of freedom to a formula, or the *closeness* to a mathematical percentage. Good translations are works of art. And good translations are rare.

In nonfiction the author is trying to convey concepts, whether in history, science, philosophy, literary criticism, economics, or other disciplines. Here a translator must have a maximum degree of precision. An essayist deals with ideas, which are fragile. Their validity and meaning depend on the underlying background, and the spirit that the translator must catch relates to the entire cultural and intellectual framework on which the ideas rest. To be sure, no two persons will have the same insight into the culture of a period. Since the degree and character of the insight form the basis of any interpretation, translators will offer differing interpretations. Such a difference is just as inescapable as the variation between individuals.

The translator must be thoroughly familiar with the background of the subject and convey the ideas with the utmost possible precision. Insertions must be minimal, limited chiefly to situations wherein a single word in the foreign language may require several English words to convey the sense. Similarly, the translator must not make deletions from the original unless, again, several of the foreign words can be rendered by a single English word.

I will give two different translations of a Latin passage, originally written by Francis Bacon early in the seventeenth century. Bacon was dealing with what we would now call scientific method and the establishment of scientific truth. He emphasized the collection of data, but insisted that the data be reliable. The philosopher David Hume, writing in the early eighteenth century, translated as follows (I quote only the first two sentences):

> We ought to make a collection or particular history of all monsters and prodigious births or productions, and in a word of every thing new, rare, and extraordinary in nature. But this must be done with the most severe scrutiny, lest we depart from truth.

Hume was an excellent English stylist and his choice of words is admirable. Yet we have no difficulty in detecting a definite eighteenth-century flavor.

The most widely used translation of Bacon today is that by Spedding, Ellis, and Heath. They offer the following translation of the passage in question:

> For we have to make a collection or particular natural history of all prodigies and monstrous births of nature; of everything in short that is in nature new, rare, and unusual. This must be done however with the strictest scrutiny, that fidelity may be ensured.

The sense is the same, but the flavor is different. Both translations are close to the original but they exhibit different shadings.

A reading knowledge of one or more foreign languages is widespread among educated Americans, very few of whom, however, will ever have occasion to publish a translation into English. Yet close attention to problems of translation will be extremely helpful to those who want to improve their skills in English composition. Merely comparing a published translation with the foreign original is valuable, but the truly rewarding exercise is to take two different translations of the same foreign text and compare them with each other and with the original. The two English renditions will certainly diverge—sometimes to such a degree that they scarcely seem to be rendering the same passage. But even if the two are fairly close and the differences between them subtle, a student will gain vast critical appreciation if he will study those differences, weigh each word in relation to the context, and judge for himself which translation is preferable—and why. He may even find that neither of them is really satisfactory.

The effort involved in all this may be considerable, but the reward will be a sharpened appreciation of context. This single word can epitomize all the problems of writing: *What is the right word in this context?* The right word is the one that gives that sense of aesthetic fit that I noted earlier, the satisfaction that marks the successful completion of an artistic effort. Exercises of this type will help the student appreciate the value of words in relation to context. And this, I suggest, is the central problem in the art of writing.

· 11 ·

Epilogue: The Keys
to the Kingdom

In the title of this chapter the word *Kingdom* indicates the primary goal that writers pursue—publication. This by itself, however, is not enough, for authors also want their works to be read and appreciated. Writers feel that they have something to say. They are not willing merely to present their ideas to the winds or the waves nor, like St. Francis, to preach their message to the birds. Instead, they want to enshrine their thoughts in print, impress particular persons, and achieve some sort of human interaction.

Orientation

Since all this involves a whole chain of individuals, interacting in different ways, a loose schema can provide a framework for discussion. First, of course, come the authors, who are trying to express themselves. Next on the scene are the evaluators and the decision makers, including the editors and referees. Then there come the concrete producers—the publishers. Next will be the purchasers and the readers, categories that overlap but are by no means identical. I would then add the critics; and, as a final stage, the historians. This schema applies to both journal articles and books.

The problems of the authors, already discussed in previous chapters, I will not pursue further. I will focus, instead, on what I consider the most important concept, *evaluation*, which comes into play at different levels and stages. Key figures are the editors, often assisted by subsidiary decision makers who, whether rightly or wrongly, are now generally called peer reviewers. The editors, however, are employees of the publishers, who face their own knotty problems. These range widely, and include both financial matters and overall policies. In some circumstances profit can be a principal motive. Yet even when this is the case, many organizations center their policies around ideologic considerations. This, perhaps, is especially true of strongly organized professional groups.

The publisher would correspond, perhaps, to the producer of a motion picture, who establishes policies and foots all the bills. The editor would then be comparable to the director of the movie. The editor, as an employee of the publisher, has the tasks of carrying out the major policies and keeping within certain budgetary limits. The editor, of course, with his own special skills, ordinarily would have his own policies which to some extent he is encouraged to implement. But if his ideas conflict with those of the publisher, difficulties arise and can influence decisions on individual manuscripts. If conflicts are severe, there will soon be a new editor.

Publication without readers is totally fruitless. A message in print, if not read, might just as well be laid before the birds. Publishers are especially concerned with sales. With journals, sales ordinarily take the form of subscriptions, a rather special form of vending. Since a journal has many separate contributions, the question arises, To what extent are any of them actually read? Publishers and editors try to find out, but with only questionable success. Nevertheless, subscription figures hold paramount importance for publishers, while the actual readership is much more problematical. Sometimes the number of "Letters to the editor" provide an extremely rough gauge.

With books, the situation is somewhat different. Here, as with any other article of commerce, sales figures give a reasonable idea of popularity. And, within limits, these figures will correlate reasonably well with the degree to which a book is read. Of the many factors that relate to sales (of books), I will pay special attention to the critical appraisal, ordinarily expressed in book reviews. Book reviewing, however, is only a special function of criticism and we must also be concerned with its wider ranges. In its broader senses, criticism affects all aspects of the writing process.

Finally, in overall evaluation, the historians provide the ultimate stage. Their judgments do not immediately influence the activities of writing or publishing but do play a significant part in shaping critical opinion. The historian, who provides an overview, affects the process of writing only indirectly.

Criticism

Most commonly the word criticism implies fault-finding, so that the phrase, "I have no criticism to make" has come to mean, "I have no fault to find." This, however, is only a limited usage that ignores the various cognate terms and their contexts. *Criticism, critic,* and *crisis* all derive from the same Greek root, *krisis.* A crisis is a turning point at which the course of events will go irretrievably in one direction or another. Earlier physicians paid a great deal of attention to the crisis in lobar pneumonia, the point of decisive change following which the patient would go on either to recovery or death. Today we have a good understanding of the mechanisms involved, but long before physicians understood the physiopathology, they could recognize the clinical phenomenon.

The Greek root of *crisis* indicates a decision or judgment, and the verb form means to judge or decide. With pneumonia, Nature had made the decision, but in other situations human judgment determines the outcome. Criticism is the act of judging, or making decisions, and a critic is a judge.

Judgments depend on standards and values, explicit or implicit. Today it is chiefly the philosopher who makes values explicit. Yet everyone has implicit values, and tends to regard as good whatever conforms thereto, and as bad whatever is discordant. For example, when people who do not like modern art declare, "I do not know much about art, but I know what I like," they are giving us a whole miniature treatise on criticism.

Such persons are indeed censorious but they are not acting as critics. Their values, the bases for their judgments, are not explicit. In ordinary usage the critic—the judge—has special knowledge and qualifications and is well acquainted with the standards on which a deliberate judgment must rest. We thus distinguish between a critical judgment based on knowledge of standards and a casual reaction of aversion or attraction.

168

The real critic knows the standards on which a judgment will rest and applies them to a particular case. At a higher level he deliberately tries to expand, elaborate, and make explicit the grounds on which a judgment is based. He thus actually helps to create standards which he and others will then apply. If we combine these two senses, we can regard criticism as the aggregate endeavor to identify, apply, and also disseminate such standards. It is indeed a noble function that far transcends mere fault-finding.

In some ways criticism is perhaps comparable to a judicial system. The judge knows the law and applies it to particular cases. Judges also interpret and expound the law. As a result, it has been well said, the law is what judges say it is. While they do not create the statutes, through interpretation they do provide meaning.

The analogy must not be pushed too far. Criticism, in the sense commonly used, applies to the area usually called aesthetics, in which there are no explicit statutes but only viewpoints. Criticism would, perhaps, be more analogous to interpreting the common law (as distinguished from statute law). To some extent, as with the law, the standards for criticism are what the critics say they are. And critics, like judges, also differ in their interpretation.

Reviews

The media to which we are constantly exposed—newspapers, journals, television, radio—are constantly providing news on what is happening in art, music, literature, science, and of course, motion pictures. In addition the media generally provide evaluations, through critics who write what are loosely called reviews. The critics or reviewers, in bestowing praise and blame, thereby popularize the standards and values they happen to have. The views thus expressed, however, exert no compulsion, so that disregard of a particular opinion ordinarily carries no penalties. We all have complete liberty to avoid a movie that has been highly recommended, buy a book that has been harshly reviewed, or disagree with an evaluation of an actor or musician.

The situation is rather different with writers who aspire to publication. They are subjected to criticism at various stages. When manuscripts are first submitted, the judgment of those critics called peer reviewers can determine their acceptance. Then, if publication does take place (for the moment considering only books, in distinction to journal articles), critical opinion may be expressed in book reviews. A book reviewer, who makes his comments after publication, bears comparison with a referee evaluating the merits of a manuscript before publication.

Book reviewers comprise an old and well established class of critics. In contrast, so-called peer reviewers represent a relatively new breed, concerned with evaluating journal articles submitted for publication, and indicating their acceptability. The book reviewer, evaluating a work already published, offers an opinion that is public, that is, printed for everyone to see. The peer reviewer, evaluating a work under consideration, offers an opinion that is private, that is, directed to the editor and kept from the author or from the public at large. Hence the peer reviewer remains anonymous.

At one time book reviews were unsigned, on the theory that greater honesty was promoted thereby. A reviewer might hesitate to sign his name to adverse comments against a person who has an established reputation or holds actual or potential power. The possibility of embarrassment, or even reprisals, of one or another sort, was by no means negligible.

However, the arguments for anonymity in book reviews now seem to have dissipated and at the present time virtually all book reviews are signed. Not only are reviewers identified by name but often there is added some information bearing on their qualifications. Many journals indicate, as part of the review, the affiliations or experience of the writer, as an indication of expertise. Such information supposedly validates competence, so that the reader of the review will have confidence in the opinion expressed. For the most part, however, the reader must take on faith the competence of the reviewer, and rely on the ability of the editor to pick appropriate critics.

With peer reviewers the anonymity remains a guarded secret, under no circumstances to be disclosed to the writer or to the eventual readers. Hence, for any published manuscript the reader has no way of judging the competence of a peer reviewer. The editors who did the choosing are sometimes proven to have been grossly mistaken.

Book reviewers and peer reviewers speak to different audiences. The former addresses the general public, especially the potential reader or purchaser; the latter only the decision maker, or editor. The former expresses himself in print in a permanent public record; the latter, almost always, remains anonymous, known only to the editor and the editorial board.

Some Problems of Book Reviewing

Every year thousands of new books are published, and vast numbers of review copies are distributed to journals. However, the space available for reviews is in short supply and so too are competent reviewers. The book publishers, recognizing this and eager to get whatever publicity they can, often send out, with the review copies, special "releases." These contain predigested information that a reviewer might use. With the help of such information, almost anyone with some journalistic skill, can "review" books, with only a minimum degree of expertise.

Since book reviewers may be hard to find, editors, when recruiting such help, often send out "directions," indicating the points to be covered or commented on. This is a sort of reviewing by formula, comparable to checking a questionnaire, and a way of making an "instant critic." Journalism of this type produces not book reviews, in the classical sense, but only extended book notices. In large part, it must be admitted, such notices prove reasonably satisfactory. They indicate the contents of the book, offer some sort of rapid evaluation, and may rouse the interest of their readers. Moreover, by giving publicity, they satisfy the book publishers.

On the other hand, many journals hold much closer to the ideals of criticism. The reviews of this type, often taking the form of essays, provide a careful evaluation and in addition place the work in the perspective of current trends. Such essays take up much more space than brief notices. Moreover, they may be quite specialized and interest only a small group of readers. But here we rely on the judgment of the editor, who must decide whether the book is truly significant. If it is, a detailed critique will make manifest that significance and justify the amount of space devoted to it.

A sound criticism must be distinguished from pedantry. In some scholarly journals the reviewers are more concerned with displaying their own erudition than with giving an objective evaluation. This self-aggrandizement, often taking the form of so-called nit-picking, is a curse of book reviewing and indicates the dry rot that has overtaken much of academia. It is far removed from true criticism.

The "Peer Review"

Before discussing the peer reviewing of journal manuscripts, I will comment briefly on the evaluation of book manuscripts. Some scholarly publishers engage in admirable practices when considering acceptance of a manuscript—a commitment not to be entered into lightly. An editor, although able to sniff out merit, must seek experts to provide real critical evaluation. Finding such experts may entail much difficulty. The success of a press can depend largely on the efforts of the editor in this regard.

Sound evaluation, when obtained, will indicate the significance of the work, the merits and weaknesses, and the ways in which these latter can be remedied. Most authors, despite their sometimes resentful first reaction, will appreciate the value of a thoughtful critical review. Sound criticism can help an author realize his potential and eventually lead to revision (or revisions) that will yield true excellence. There is a great satisfaction when—as occasionally occurs—an author's preface acknowledges an indebtedness to the anonymous reviewers who helped shape the finished work. This we can regard as peer review at its best.

On the other hand, some manuscripts, subjected to the peer review process and eventually published, receive highly adverse book reviews. A single one may reflect only a personal bias, but multiple unfavorable notices will cast doubt on the validity of the original peer review. To be sure, critics, like judges, disagree. There is no single canon of truth. Pluralism reigns among values, and only the historian, in retrospection, will eventually bring order into the conflicts.

Many persons believe that the same type of peer review used to evaluate book manuscripts should also apply to journal articles. We may appropriately ask the simple question, Why? What is the real point of having so-called peer review journals that engage in such practices? Although the question seems simple, any possible answers would be exceedingly complex, and can be approached only through a historical account. Fortunately, historian John Burnham has recently provided a truly landmark survey of the whole peer review process and the way it developed [1]. His excellent account makes certain points of special relevance to our discussion.

There was no single or direct route whereby this procedure of peer review either came into being or spread. The many different kinds of journals, published under highly variable conditions by different types of editors, render impossible any simple generalization. Some editors were quite autocratic regarding acceptance of manuscripts, others, even at an early stage of medical journalism, accepted and even sought consultation. Some journals were privately owned, so that the editor and publisher were the same individual. In others the publisher was some organization, which entrusted the conduct of the journal to an editor, often with an editorial board. For the most part the editor would rely on his own knowledge, but in particular cases where further expertise was desirable, he would consult with his editorial board or seek independent advice.

For the present analysis the crucial feature was the relatively modest number of satisfactory manuscripts submitted for publication. Editors often had difficulty in filling their pages and had to scurry to get enough papers. An editorial board was expected to solicit manuscripts and act as a source of supply through their own contacts. Even when there was an adequate number of submissions, as in the larger journals whose pages could be reasonably well supplied by papers read at annual meetings, an editor could depend on his own competence and judgment or on his in-house staff.

There was little need to go outside, and the personality of the editor, sometimes of colossal egotism, might hold this need to a minimum.

The increasing complexity of science, with resulting specialization, was another major factor in change. (Here I am referring especially to medical science and practice, where alone I can speak from personal knowledge.) Expansion of technology, coupled with elaboration of new concepts, created new fields of expertise. We recall that Francis Bacon, in the seventeenth century, took all knowledge to be his province. By the mid-twentieth century, however, no single individual could take as his province even a quite limited area of medicine.

Accompanying specialization was a vastly increased amount of research, with the resulting increased number of manuscripts seeking publication. Burnham points out that as the twentieth century progressed, editors had to select from a greater abundance of worthwhile material and had to sift out the best from a mass that was substantially good. Scarcity of good papers gave way to glut, so that choice became increasingly difficult. The process was intensified when highly specialized and esoteric techniques were involved, with the result that the ability to pass judgment was possessed by relatively few. Consultation became more and more urgent.

If existing journals could not cope with all the good manuscripts pressing for acceptance, one partial solution was the establishment of new and more specialized journals to publish them. But this was not the real answer. New modes of evaluation became a pressing need. In this environment the institution of peer review gradually took shape, to become more and more prevalent during the third quarter of the century. ·

Elitism Among Journals

Medical journals form a key link in the dissemination of new knowledge, which in turn serves to fuel the entire health industry. With the vast increase in manuscripts seeking publication and of journals to publish them, the question of evaluation becomes pressing indeed. An assertion appearing in print is not necessarily true. How to judge the reliability of what any particular journal publishes?

We find a comparable difficulty in trying to estimate the reliability of a medical practitioner. This perennial problem, acute for many centuries, has been "solved" many times, but unfortunately no solutions have lasted very long. Educated practitioners tried to set themselves apart from the uneducated and claimed their levels of education and experience as a touchstone of competence. Medical history reveals the successive attempts whereby particular groups tried to establish themselves as a true elite, worthy of special privileges.

For a brief period state licensing seemed to be the answer. When this failed, different kinds of societies, academies, and associations sprang up, arrogating to themselves certain privileges in accordance with traditional guild practice. Corresponding to these organizations various specialties appeared, whose members provided their own criteria for validation. The so-called specialty boards publicized the concept of particular competence in designated areas. However, specialties multiplied so rapidly that soon virtually everyone became a specialist of one or another sort. Need for still a higher form of elitism was emerging.

The analogy to medical journalism is, I think, close. As the practitioners had already done, some medical journals wanted to distance themselves from less reliable competitors. To do so they wanted to validate their merits through some sort of explicit standards—a form of certification. By the mid-twentieth century the answer seemed to be the new and plausible criterion of peer review. It was an invitation to jump on the bandwagon of elitism.

To be a peer review journal meant that manuscripts published therein had won the approval not merely of the editor, but also of special reviewers who allegedly had an expertise equal to that of the author. The word *peer* is dreadfully unfortunate in this regard. Deriving from the Latin *par*, equal, it stresses the concept of equality. The usage also has a subtle implication that the editor is not equal to the task of evaluation and so he must call upon peers who would really be the equals.

The absurdity of all this becomes clear if we examine the actual meaning of the words. We cannot have equality in general but must specify the particular respects. The word *peer* originally referred to politics and government, since different social classes had different civil status. If the members of a group all had equal status and condition, they were peers, equal to each other, but not necessarily to other groups. By usage, the term *peers* came to be applied to the higher social groups, particularly the nobility.

In science the qualities that identify peers are, of course, not social status but knowledge and skill. How can these be determined in any given instance? Are all the members of a given specialty truly peers? Or are all authors who have published in the same general field? They might share considerable knowledge, but this might be vastly inferior to the expertise of a given author who submits a manuscript.

Editors, pondering acceptance of a manuscript, may lack sufficient background for proper evaluation and therefore seek consultation with persons of more specialized knowledge. In editorial work such reliance on knowledgeable consultants is a time-honored practice. Indeed, at the present time almost any journal can legitimately say, "The editor and the editorial staff, whenever necessary, use outside consultants before reaching a decision." To what extent does this statement differ from the claim of being a peer review journal? Crucial here, of course, is the meaning assigned to the word "necessary" and the amount and type of consultation.

Two distinct difficulties attend the concept of peer review, namely, the nature of the peer and the nature of the review. For the moment let us attend to the latter and the distinction between a review and a consultation. An editorial consultation, I suggest, is comparable to a consultation in clinical medicine. The editor makes clear the problems on which expert advice is sought. In editorial practice each manuscript would be individualized and its special problems identified. The editor may, for example, be favorably impressed by its overall quality but unsure whether the technology is adequate or the statistical data sound. Consultation with suitable experts may resolve his doubts.

At an opposite extreme the editor may have no adequate familiarity with the subject matter and may feel quite unable to offer a legitimate opinion. In such cases the prudent editor asks some truly knowledgeable person to act as *ad hoc* editor and to provide a complete evaluation, with recommendations for disposition. The complexities of modern medicine render this course increasingly necessary.

By analogy with clinical medicine, if the first mode resembles consultation, the second is referral of the patient to a specialist who then provides evaluation and recommendations for treatment. However, in this rough analogy there is a third category, namely, the patients for whom the clinician, together with his office associates, take complete responsibility without seeking outside opinions. The editor and his in-house staff are quite comparable, I believe, to such a clinical group.

A peer review journal might seem to be boasting that every published manuscript, regardless of its character, has received a second opinion. This, I suggest, might be comparable to the physician in practice who never treats a patient before getting a second opinion, and even makes a boast of this. It does not speak well for the competence of the physician.

When a second opinion is considered obligatory, manuscripts are not really individualized. The editors routinely scurry around to find someone who, at least on paper, might appear qualified to pass judgment. There is no real consultation on particular features. Instead they may be offered a check list to cover such topics as validity, originality, importance, interest, clarity, and overall quality. Some sort of commentary would also be expected, in whatever length and detail the reviewer might wish. In the evaluative process a check list is the complete nadir. It ignores the individuality and special problems of any manuscript, and these the editor should identify and evaluate.

Bureaucratic routine can easily replace reliance on editorial insight and ability. The frequent need for consultation is not at issue. At issue is only the merit of the routinized and formalized process of consultation, mistakenly called "peer review" and heralded as a virtue.

A rigid requirement of getting outside opinions suggests that the editorial staff is inexperienced and perhaps mediocre and not too trustworthy. Obligatory outside review then represents a crutch without which the journal could not function. Use of this crutch involves enormous expenditure of time and effort. An alternative would be to improve the quality of the editors. Great journals are created by great editors, who know when, and where, and how to find consultants, when necessary. Weak editors can speedily run a journal into the ground.

The Historian's Insight

Can a routine system, automatically applied, substitute for individual excellence that is not systematized?

Francis Bacon, in the early seventeenth century, claimed that this could be done. He had contributed much to our modern notions of scientific method. He emphasized the importance of facts and of suitable means of ascertaining them. By collecting enough data and setting them out in the proper relationships, he thought that truth would emerge. He was trying to provide a routine method of achieving validity.

The details (for which the reader must go to the text of his famous *New Organon*) are not important here. Important is his belief that a suitable routine could produce a uniform result that would not be affected by differences in individual ability. He declared, "For my way of discovering sciences goes far to level men's wits, and leaves but little to individual excellence; because it performs everything by the surest rules and demonstrations" [2]. Rules and demonstrations, he thought, could eliminate the need for individual excellence and place all wits on a level.

Can rules, however detailed, substitute for "individual excellence"? Or does progress depend on individual excellence and the implied difference in wits? Instead of offering an answer, I return to the problems of publication. Does not the current emphasis on "peer review" follow the views of Francis Bacon, by trying to substitute a bureaucratic routine for the excellence of individual editors?

References
1. Burnham, J. The evolution of the editorial peer review. JAMA 1323–1329, 1990.
2. Bacon, F. In *The New Organon*, Book I, Aphorism cxxii.

Index